W9-CXP-050

Nimble Documentation®

Also available from ASQ Quality Press

Managing Records for ISO 9000 Compliance
Eugenia K. Brumm

Documenting Quality for ISO 9000 and Other Industry Standards
Gary E. MacLean

Eight-Step Process to Successful ISO 9000 Implementation:
A Quality Management System Approach
Lawrence A. Wilson

Understanding and Applying Value-Added Assessment:
Eliminating Business Process Waste
William E. Trischler

Human Resources Management Perspectives on TQM: Concepts and Practices
Stephen B. Knouse, editor

To request a complimentary catalog of publications, call 800-248-1946.

Nimble Documentation®

The Practical Guide for World-Class Organizations

Adrienne Escoe

ASQ Quality Press
Milwaukee, Wisconsin

Nimble Documentation®: The Practical Guide for World-Class Organizations
Adrienne Escoe

Library of Congress Cataloging-in-Publication Data
Escoe, Adrienne.
    Nimble documentation: the practical guide for world-class
organizations / Adrienne Escoe.
      p. cm.
    Includes bibliographical references and index.
    ISBN 0-87389-423-5 (alk. paper)
    1. Quality control—Documentation. I. Title.
TS156.E78   1997
658.5'62—dc21   97-15785
                                          CIP

Trademark Acknowledgment
Many of the designations used by manufacturers and sellers to distinguish their products are claimed as trademarks. Where these designations appear in this book and ASQ Quality Press was aware of a trademark claim, the designations have been printed in initial caps.

Nimble Documentation is registered with the U.S. Patent and Trademark Office and owned by Adrienne Escoe.

10 9 8 7 6 5 4 3 2 1

ISBN 0-87389-423-5

Acquisitions Editor: Roger Holloway
Project Editor: Jeanne W. Bohn

ASQ Mission: To facilitate continuous improvement and increase customer satisfaction by identifying, communicating, and promoting the use of quality principles, concepts, and technologies; and thereby be recognized throughout the world as the leading authority on, and champion for, quality.

Attention: Schools and Corporations
ASQ Quality Press books, videotapes, audiotapes, and software are available at quantity discounts with bulk purchases for business, educational, or instructional use. For information, please contact ASQ Quality Press at 800-248-1946, or write to ASQ Quality Press, P.O. Box 3005, Milwaukee, WI 53201-3005.

For a free copy of the ASQ Quality Press Publications Catalog, including ASQ membership information, call 800-248-1946.

Printed in the United States of America

 Printed on acid-free paper

American Society for Quality

ASQ™

Quality Press
611 East Wisconsin Avenue
Milwaukee, Wisconsin 53202

To Matthew and Jennifer
and the power of Divine Love.

Good happens.

Contents

Part IV Information Tools

Tables, Figures, and Checklists

Tables

Figures

Checklists

Foreword

In the swiftly changing realm of global business, every aspect of an organization's operations must be continually evaluated and refocused to ensure alliance with its strategic objectives and an increasingly competitive environment. Frequently neglected, documentation is left to form as it always has, or to be reformed as a byproduct of each unique program or product line.

This book establishes documentation in a proper perspective, helping leaders use it as a resource to reach an organization's goals faster and to stay proactive to the needs of its markets and employees. Following the book's guidelines allows organizations to determine the specific policies and procedures relevant to their objectives and environment, to develop them and maintain them economically, and to take advantage of technology to make documentation readily accessible.

I had the privilege to observe, firsthand, the success of the author's approach to zero-based documentation at a major international company. I saw the positive, measurable impact of a documentation center of excellence, including the development of a team of skilled, responsive employees.

For my business of process reengineering and enablement through technology insertion, *Nimble Documentation*® provides the practical advice needed on how to facilitate and sustain change in the critical domain of business documentation. I welcome this book to our repository of best practices.

Diane M. Galusky
Director, Systems Delivery
Computer Sciences Corporation

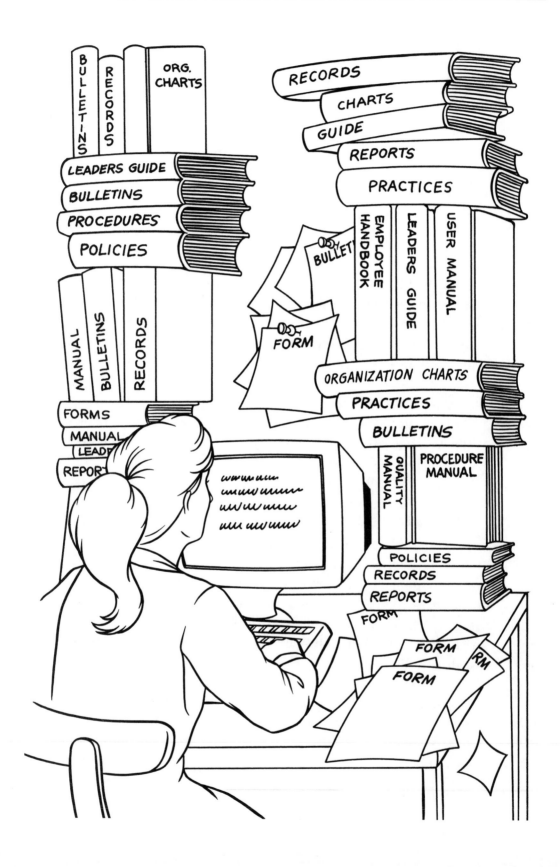

Preface

This book is a practical guide for streamlining, producing, and managing documentation from ISO 9001-compliant policies to work instructions, from process maps to forms, from employee handbooks to user manuals. It is for world-class organizations—companies whose constant and competitive process improvement mirrors their responsiveness to customers and the global marketplace. These are organizations that can afford only trim, current, and accessible documents that add value and are people-friendly. They seek every advantage of technology, such as standardized hardware and software, imaging, and intranets. This book is also for organizations that may be on the cutting edge of their industries, yet have let their documentation systems grow mold. Their cumbersome and obsolete procedures and handbooks can snub customers and suffocate employees—and may be a resource bomb waiting to be detonated by the next legal challenge.

How is *Nimble Documentation*® different from other resources? Traditional systems and procedures (S&P) textbooks, although useful for basic guidance in document hierarchies and structures, typically do not address a wide range of applications, such as quality standards, employee handbooks, and safety programs. They do not deal with human issues, such as self-directed teams, or with continuous measured improvement. How-to books tend to focus on a small slice of the subject, for example, ISO 9000 documentation or records. Other books center on technology issues such as electronic searching, and generally are written for technical users. Many titles are available on format and style, but none highlights the advantages and disadvantages of various ones according to the specific needs of competitive organizations. This volume brings all of these elements together in a single, nontechnical, integrated resource.

This book has many features for a wide range of readers. One major benefit is the concept of zero-based documentation and the litmus test for developing or streamlining documentation. "This test is a clear and compelling analytical framework for rooting out old, useless documents and records and is greatly needed by most, if not all, organizations throughout the world. It is a way of thinning the weeds that have grown in most organizations and turning an overgrown field of organizational activity into a neatly trimmed garden." Another main benefit is the section on format. It gives readers a "valuable set of comparison criteria for developing various types of documentation and serves as a checklist for evaluating current documents and records." The section on style guides readers to recognize the importance of stylistic conventions as a prerequisite to effective communication in today's global organizations. It gives them a tool for meeting the needs of diverse personnel. Also, the chapter on measured improvement helps the many organizations that are struggling to get a grip on their documentation and that often have no idea how to measure the progress of those efforts. The criteria, techniques, and methods described in this chapter assist all types of organizations to develop clear goals and objectives for documentation revision efforts and allow them to determine how well they are documenting and recording organizational learning.

A wide variety of industries and virtually any type of organization can gain much from this book. Information-intensive industries, such as health care, software development, publishing, and Internet service providers, can especially profit from it. The book offers much to a broad spectrum of readers, such as quality assurance personnel, S&P staff, operations managers, production personnel, writers, records administrators, librarians and archivists, employee and organizational development facilitators, business and technical writing faculty and students, and process improvement consultants.

Nimble Documentation® is a guidebook, with illustrations pertaining to real business situations drawn primarily from experiences at one of the world's largest companies, but also from many organizations of all sizes across varied industries—manufacturing and service industries as well as public agencies. Simple diagrams, metrics, format examples, and other graphics illustrate key concepts throughout. Checklists provide practical road maps.

The book's foundation is documentation need—including legal requirements, external customers, users, subject matter owners, and certification auditors and examiners—and the concept of zero-based documentation. Although readers can find solutions to many kinds of documentation challenges throughout the book, reading Chapters 1 and 2 first provides a useful trail head for exploring any of the other chapters. Chapter 1, Introduction, presents a framework for the book and a useful section, Using This Book, Chapter 2, Zero-Based Documentation, describes the litmus test and a case study. The organization of the book supports readers who are seeking to establish a new documentation system or streamline an old one. Subsequent chapters are grouped by *Implementation, Application,* and *Information Tools.* To further assist readers, each chapter through Chapter 9 begins with examples of solutions presented in that chapter. Appendices are home to performance criteria for S&P personnel.

[Quotations in the preface are from Anton Camarota, a reviewer.]

Acknowledgments

Thank you to so many people for your inspiration, opportunities to work with your organizations, assistance, and permission to reference your accomplishments in *Nimble Documentation*®: *The Practical Guide for World-Class Organizations,* including the policies and practices team at The Aerospace Corporation; Roxana Alford; Annette Baumgartner; Tracy Bermasconi; Jeanne Bohn; Jeff Borges; Dr. Donna Born; James Briscoe; Stacy Buckley; Bill Caldwell; David Cole; Grayson Cook; Tom Dale; Carol Davis; Jennifer Ervin; Mike Flanagan; Normand Frigon; Zizi Gibbs; Tracy and John Giovannoni; Michael Goodger; Susan Henderson; Rod Hennington; Roger Holloway; the systems and procedures, forms, and records management teams at Hughes Electronics; the team at Insulation Supply Company; Harry Jackson, Jr.; Susan Krell; Hazelina Belladora-Laskey; Dr. Harris Lehrer; Don Leonard; Kimberly Manthey; Linda Masquefa; John Montaña; Norman Nelson; Ann Niese; Dr. George Paulikas; John Phillips; Chuck Porter; Phyllis Price; Edith Shanahan; Donald Skupsky; Kristen Smith; Terry Strauss-Thacker; Kibbee Streetman; the team at Superior Thread Rolling Company; Raymond Urgo; Annette Wall; and everyone else whose name was omitted in my eagerness to get out the word.

Extra special thanks go to Anton Camarota, Kathleen Glasgow, and Melvin Smith, whose thorough reviews of the book's early drafts helped to strengthen it tremendously.

PART I

Need

CHAPTER 1

Introduction

> Solutions presented in this chapter address documentation challenges such as
>
> - What is the purpose of this book?
> - What is Nimble Documentation®?
> - Who can this book help?
> - How to find information in this book

A. Nimbleness

Have you heard the *thud test* for evaluating documentation quality? A board member recently opened a chapter meeting of the Society for Technical Communication with the following story.

> *I asked a technical writer how one of her major clients judged the quality of her work.*
>
> *"Oh, that's easy" answered the writer confidently. "They rely on the thud test."*
>
> *"What's that?" I asked.*
>
> *"After completing each manual, I drop it on the floor," the writer said matter-of-factly. "The louder the thud, the happier the client."*

Although some people measure document quality by weight or volume, many more understand the liabilities of documentation that is too many, too long, and too wordy (see Figure 1.1). These people know that documentation must be clear, concise, current, and accessible. They recognize that world-class companies and public agencies cannot afford inflexible policies and procedures manuals, operating practices that lead to rework, or records that build liability.

Nimble Documentation® is a practical guide to trim, flexible, and accessible documentation for world-class organizations. It focuses on sources of need—external customers, users, subject matter owners, and others—and addresses measured, integrated improvement and electronic alternatives, including storage and retrieval systems, local area networks (LANs), and the Internet. This is a guidebook for organizations that have too much documentation, those that don't have enough, and those that have the wrong kind. It is for organizations that take too long and spend too much money on communicating information. From a zero-based approach to illustrative applications and practical ideas for liberating documentation relatives, such as approval authority systems, this book is an organization's comprehensive resource for responsive written media.

This book is a reference for organizations and individuals responsible for

- Drafting, coordinating, reviewing, publishing (hard copy and electronically), managing, or purchasing business documentation, including policies, practices, procedures, instructions, records, forms, or approval authority systems

- Leading an organization through a quality initiative, such as ISO 9000, or applying for the Malcolm Baldrige National Quality Award

- Improving operating and management processes

- Preparing for or conducting audits

- Purchasing software to develop business documentation

- Training those responsible for business documentation

- Making documentation staffing decisions

- Saving money and time

- Empowering teams

- Designing on-line documentation systems

- Developing employee handbooks, user manuals, safety programs, and other documentation

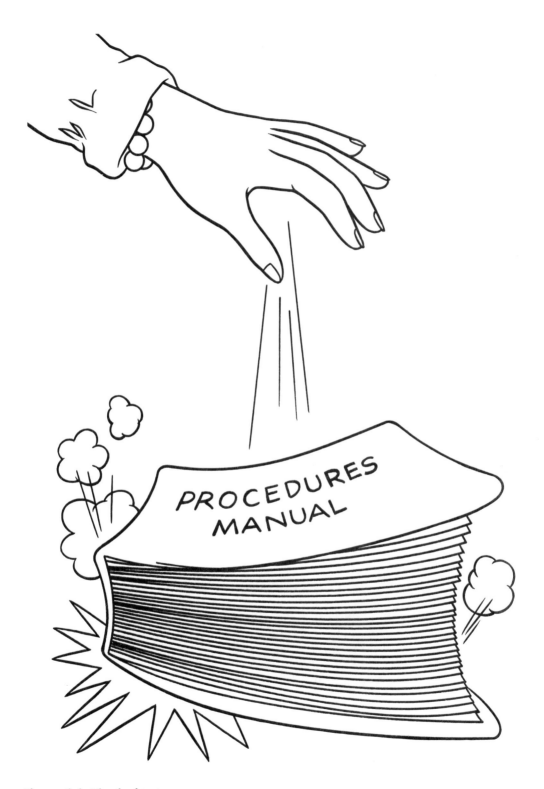

Figure 1.1. The thud test.

Nimble Documentation® flunks thud tests. It is far away from thunder-thud manuals and wearying wordiness. Nimble Documentation® meets minimum requirements for legal, contractual, and business goals. It means information that helps organizations respond quickly to changing market and workplace conditions and doesn't impede business. Nimble Documentation® is easy to access and economical to maintain. It is there when you need it and out of the way when you don't. It can be readily revised, is portable, and suits world-class organizations, which respond quickly to customers and other sources of need, jump operational hurdles, are allergic to waste, stimulate employees, and thrive on continuous constructive change.

Documentation has many meanings, from the broad—anything written in any medium—to the narrow—policies and procedures manuals or perhaps records.

Nimble Documentation® needs to be clear, lean, current, and accessible. First, let's consider some examples of documentation that *isn't* nimble.

1. An electronics company's policies and practices manual that includes internal operating procedures for every department whose manager believed a procedure would secure the department's existence during downsizing

2. A financial software user's guide that buries critical troubleshooting steps in wordy narrative paragraphs

3. A distributor's human resources requisition form that requires eight original signatures, half of which belong to off-site managers and executives

4. A state government's 350-page service guide capped by a one-page index

5. An international defense division's memorandum distributed widely to communicate signature authority for committing company funds

6. Bulletins and announcements issued in immediate response to various audits yet in effect for decades

All of these examples demonstrate documentation that is unnecessary, hard to access, time-consuming to process, obsolete, incomplete, or resource-gobbling. None of the examples support an organization's responsiveness to rapidly changing conditions—inside or out, internal administration or marketplace. All can sabotage the best efforts of an agile company or one aspiring to be.

In all the preceding examples, the perspective is the writer's, creator's, or documentation's sponsor. It is not the user's, the reader's, or the person who maintains, reviews, or approves it. If a document is created, revised, or maintained according to the writer or sponsor's needs or goals, the battle for nimbleness will be uphill. If such a document *does* achieve nimbleness, the accomplishment will be accidental. On the other hand, documents, and the processes surrounding them, designed genuinely from the user's point of view seldom will be cumbersome or slow, assuming skilled implementation of the design and the sponsoring organization's commitment to nimbleness.

Few people read business documentation for recreation. They read it for solutions, which they want quickly.

Take the first example. An employee wants to get something printed by an in-house print shop. She doesn't want to and doesn't have time to search a manual for a company procedure written primarily to secure the print shop's rectangle on an organization chart. The employee's needs would be served better by brief instructions placed at the service counter, where the transaction will take place. That is where the information will be applied.

The software user, in the second example, needs to locate information immediately. Payroll deadlines demand it. What is the solution? Replace the narrative writing with modular instructions that facilitate quick access to information (see Chapter 3).

Approving the multiple-signature form (the third example) takes too long. Anyhow, the last, or last few, signatures represent the only people who actually will read the requisition. Everyone else assumes the next person will. Honesty and capable management dictate that reviewers formally assign authority to the lowest-level employee who has the knowledge and skills to approve the requisition. Another alternative is to use an electronic approval system to speed along the transaction (see Chapter 8).

If documentation were created from the user's perspective in examples 4 through 6, it could be transformed in some way to achieve nimbleness.

Consider a few other examples, where documentation is created from the user's perspective.

7. A national charity's three-year-old telephone directory that includes fax numbers and e-mail addresses

8. A high-tech machine shop's on-line procedures that do not list related documents and forms, but instead rely on electronic searching

9. A chemical company's combination safety training needs assessment/training record that eliminates duplicate data entry

10. An automobile after-market product manufacturer that uses video work instructions, compliant with the ISO 9001 standard, for its multilingual workforce

11. A food processor's functional records retention schedule that specifies an easy-to-maintain records inventory

Many examples in this book illustrate how world-class companies pay attention to document users and other sources of need.

B. The Framework

Nimble Documentation® is achieved through subjecting it (whether proposed or existing) to a litmus test. Before any piece is added to a documentation system—for example, a new manual, procedure, form, paragraph, or phrase—or before a streamlining effort, it is evaluated from a zero base. That means no piece is accepted into the system unless it can be proven to meet clearly defined needs, or its exclusion can be shown to cause possible harm to the organization. In Chapter 2, five sources of need are defined: legal requirements, external customers, users, subject matter owners, and certification auditors and examiners. A source of need can be anyone, or any requirement, for whom a service is furnished or to whom a product is delivered. An example would be an administrator who follows a user manual developed for a company's new human resources (HR) system. Another source of need is a law requiring a published statement that prohibits workplace harassment. And yet another is to reconstruct a business after a disaster such as a fire, tornado, flood, or earthquake.

Litmus test criteria for Nimble Documentation® can be stated as questions to assess the need for any piece of documentation. In one form or another, the questions focus on legal, contractual, or prudent business requirements (which can originate from several sources), and the harm that might come to an organization if the documentation were never created. Chapter 2 addresses sources of need and the litmus test for Nimble Documentation®.

C. Using This Book

Nimble Documentation® follows a practical chronology for developing a documentation system from scratch or streamlining an existing system. Four major topic groups divide the sequence: *Need, Implementation,*

Application, and *Information Tools.* Individual topics, chapters within each topic group, are developed fully and can be used as stand-alone references to help solve a single or immediate problem; however, readers who consult with only a portion of this book are encouraged to first read at least enough of Chapter 2 to understand the advantages and approach of zero-based documentation. This foundation will help readers make sound choices for implementing and applying the concepts. The book suggests solutions for many types of documentation challenges, such as to reduce the size of a policies and practices manual (Chapter 2), format a procedure (Chapter 3), calculate documentation costs, including hidden resource drains (Chapter 5), make a user manual user-friendly (Chapter 7), and weigh the advantages and disadvantages of outsourcing a documentation function (Chapter 9). Figure 1.2 shows the topic groups and chapters.

The first topic group, *Need,* establishes the rationale for Nimble Documentation® and presents a useful test for deciding which documents, or their parts, to maintain and which to eliminate or avoid including in the first place.

The second, *Implementation,* guides readers to structure a documentation system, including manuals and other document collections; format individual documents; and apply writing styles that support users' goals. This topic group includes a discussion of electronic alternatives to hard copy documentation and a chapter on continuous measured improvement and metrics, such as proofreading and defect-free writing, eliminating obsolete documents, and reducing cycle time, volume, and cost.

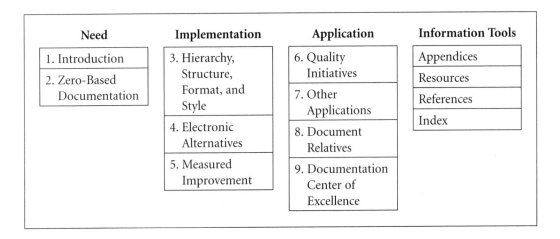

Need	**Implementation**	**Application**	**Information Tools**
1. Introduction 2. Zero-Based Documentation	3. Hierarchy, Structure, Format, and Style 4. Electronic Alternatives 5. Measured Improvement	6. Quality Initiatives 7. Other Applications 8. Document Relatives 9. Documentation Center of Excellence	Appendices Resources References Index

Figure 1.2. Chronology of *Nimble Documentation*®.

The third group, *Application,* presents three quality initiatives and their documentation requirements or implications: ISO 9000, the Baldrige Award, and total quality management (TQM). This topic group also illustrates other applications, including employee handbooks, user manuals, safety programs, ISO 14001, and more. Here, readers will also find suggestions for creating an easy-to-use records system, efficient forms, and a trim, dynamic approval authority system. The third topic group ends with comprehensive guidance for establishing a documentation center of excellence (COE), either for a large organization that centralizes documentation functions or for a firm that supplies documentation services to other companies, such as word processing or desktop publishing.

Finally, *Information Tools* equips readers with sources for additional information, including a list of organizations (and their publications and software) and a generously cross-referenced index to help locate information in *Nimble Documentation*®.

CHAPTER 2

Zero-Based Documentation

> Solutions presented in this chapter address documentation challenges such as
>
> - How to determine if documentation is really needed
> - How to apply the litmus test
> - How one organization streamlined its policies and practices

Nimble Documentation® makes life better for organizations. It meets customers' requirements and other sources of need and helps organizations respond quickly to changing market and workplace conditions. It fulfills streamlining initiatives because documentation is published or maintained only when a requirement for it is demonstrated. Chapter 2 presents the source-of-need base for documentation and a litmus test for identifying those needs. Then, the chapter takes us through a documentation streamlining success story.

A. Customers and Other Sources of Need

The saga of the *any* key is a reminder to keep the customer first in documentation. Sometimes the people who develop management information systems (MIS) are not equally skilled in documenting their systems. Sometimes highly skilled documentation specialists overlook some customers' needs or other requirements. In the late 1980s, the systems and procedures (S&P) department at Hughes Aircraft Company's Ground Systems Group spearheaded the transition to an on-line storage and retrieval system for Group management and operating practices. Near the rollout of the project, the computing and data processing department responsible for installing the mainframe system wrote user instructions. After piloting the instructions with novices, S&P decided to simplify and clarify them because many users had trouble following them.

S&P edited the step-by-step instructions so they were easy to follow and piloted them with a new group of users. One day, a pilot user called about the instructions. "I've looked everywhere," she said, "but cannot find the *any* key on my keyboard." Perplexed, an S&P staff member asked the caller to explain. "The instructions say, 'Press any key,' and I can't find the *any* key."

No matter how well we think we are meeting our customers' needs, and other sources of need, assessing success in meeting them is a documentation function's primary responsibility.

Documentation need originates from at least five sources: legal requirements, external customers, users, subject matter owners, and certification auditors and examiners.

Legal requirements. In the United States, federal and state laws dictate many processes, especially in industries and public service where health and safety are primary concerns, such as foods, pharmaceuticals, nuclear energy, transportation, and law enforcement. In fact, companies in highly regulated industries are some of the biggest consumers of documentation. Organizations in other countries are governed by national and provincial laws and sometimes by requirements adopted by international consortia, such as the European Union. State laws govern education, banking, environmental management, and many other areas of business. Laws related to employment practices exist at many levels of government. Local zoning regulations affect a company's physical facilities and are just one area of county and municipal legal sources.

External customers. Contracts with paying customers, teaming agreements, purchase orders, specification sheets, and many other written documents dictate the requirements of external customers. Conferences, meetings, and other types of communication often refine external customers' requirements. Unspoken stimuli for meeting external customers' needs, such as competitors' capabilities and benchmarked best practices, also suggest documentation. For example, a software producer packages a quick start instruction booklet with its new, competing product.

Figure 2.1. The *any* key.

In many companies, customers in other functions consult with documentation function personnel for department procedures, bulletins, memos, and other writing, editing, and documentation management projects. An S&P department of a large electronics company uses a feedback sheet to evaluate its customer service and plan corrective action if needed. The department compiles data on department service and on individual analysts' service. Figure 2.2 shows the department's feedback sheet.

Customer Service Feedback

Analyst _____ Date _____ Customer _____

Systems & Procedures would appreciate your feedback on the recent project we performed with you. Please take a few minutes to complete this survey and mail it to:

Systems & Procedures Dept.
Bldg. XY/MS A100

Thank you for the opportunity to serve you.

Are you a first-time customer of Systems & Procedures?   **Yes   No**

	Strongly Agree	Agree	Somewhat Agree	Disagree	Strongly Disagree
The analyst who assisted me was courteous.	_____	_____	_____	_____	_____
The work was performed on time.	_____	_____	_____	_____	_____
My questions regarding command media were answered to my satisfaction.	_____	_____	_____	_____	_____
The quality of work was excellent.	_____	_____	_____	_____	_____
I use command media often.	_____	_____	_____	_____	_____
I find command media understandable and useful.	_____	_____	_____	_____	_____

How can we do a better job for you?

_____

_____

_____

_____

_____

_____

Figure 2.2. Customer service feedback.

Users. A few examples of users include employees who read procedures to obtain management and operating direction, an improvement team that accesses and examines records of equipment output to redesign a part, viewers who communicate with their network provider's technical support through an interactive web site, job candidates who complete an employment application, and violators who read a statement of their rights in traffic court.

Subject matter owners. Many organizations assign responsibilities for writing, editing, word processing, and publishing to individuals, teams, or departments outside the subject matter functions. Documentation COEs (see Chapter 9) take advantage of consolidated skills, facilities, and equipment. Traditionally, functional managers have been the subject matter owners, or custodians, but new leadership structures increasingly indicate others, such as teams, for that role. Subject matter owners, typically, approve documentation before it is published, revised, or canceled.

Auditors and examiners. Quality, cleanliness, purity, financial practice, and curriculum are just a few domains subject to auditors or examiners, either external or internal. ISO 9000 series registration requires third-party auditing, although organizations often appoint internal auditors for preregistration evaluation. A few other examples are Baldrige Award examiners, registrar accreditation committees, college accreditation organizations, and scholarship application judges.

Many other sources of need apply to zero-based documentation, but the five just described are common to many industries and public services. They are summarized in Table 2.1.

How do you find out need? Review legal requirements and certification standards. Ask customers what they need in procedures. Would they prefer a "reference document" list, a list of related forms, or a particular format, such

Table 2.1. Five sources of need.

Legal requirements	Expressed as laws, regulations, and permits
External customers	Expressed as contracts, purchase orders, or specifications
Users	Personnel who read procedures to obtain management and operating direction
Subject matter owners	Company managers who are responsible for the content of the procedures
Auditors and examiners	Examples include ISO 9000 registrars, Baldrige Award examiners, and accreditation judges

as a play script or a flowchart? You can send out questionnaires; but one of the most powerful and efficient vehicles for collecting customer data is well-structured focus groups. Modify the following focus group approach according to the size of your company.

- Determine key sources of need (external customers, users, subject matter owners, and so on).
- Request their management's support for participating in the focus group meeting.
- Distribute information about the meeting a couple of weeks *before* the meeting. Include the date, time, location, agenda, and names of participants.
- Describe specific documentation issues to be discussed and ask participants to talk with others in their function or position regarding the issues.
- Appoint a facilitator and scribe to keep the meeting on track and record decisions, respectively.
- Hold a focus group meeting. Gain consensus.
- Publicize decisions to participants and their managers.
- Implement the decisions.

Useful focus group questions relate to the following aspects of documentation.

- Essential parts
- Internal format (for example, logical and comprehensive paragraph numbering)
- Quality (accuracy, currentness, and defect-free copy)
- Access (electronic or hard copy)
- Revision notification system (cover sheets and e-mail)
- Cost (processing, coordination, approval, publication, maintenance, storage, and retrieval)

Because writers rushing to meet a deadline can lose sight of their audience (their readers), a mock bumper sticker was introduced in "Analytical Writing Skills," a course developed for managers at the Los Angeles County Probation Department (see Figure 2.3). Nimble Documentation®—whether

I WRITE FOR THE READER

Figure 2.3. *I Write for the Reader* bumper sticker.

work instructions, web pages, or memos—accomplishes the writer's goals by meeting readers' needs. An operating procedure that, *to the reader,* is clear, concise, and accessible, saves time and moves the reader closer to the writer's goal. Supervisors who want their staff to review procedures for working with a new machine, for example, should keep work instructions simple and in the employees' primary language. A bank's web site designer wishing to attract viewers to her company's on-line list of CD yields presents web pages with cutting-edge graphics only if they become visible quickly on most computers. Department managers who want busy staff to know about deletions from a list of approved vendors head memos with short but complete subject lines and limit text to the minimum needed to convey essential information. Although the format and need for these examples vary widely, all are designed to help the reader get the message.

B. Litmus Test

In the late 1980s, Hughes Aircraft Company's Ground Systems Group, based in Fullerton, California, cut its three-volume practices manual from about 1000 pages to about 500. A couple of years later, it was further reduced to a single loose-leaf binder of about 350 pages. In the mid-1990s, the El Segundo, California, Aerospace Corporation slimmed its corporate policies and practices manual down by about half. How did they do it?

For as long as anyone could remember at either organization, employees saw their *command media* (a common term in the defense industry for *management and operating directive documents*) as sacred ground. The idea of eliminating any part of the mostly obsolete, cumbersome, and expensive-to-maintain manuals was routinely dismissed as an invitation for government auditors to close down the plant or administrative heresy. At best, in both cases, streamlining the command media was a low priority.

Even when executive managers approved projects to slim down the manuals and make them more accessible to users, several internal functions balked at simplifying language, eliminating redundant sections, or making the documents more accessible. In one case, the president announced at his staff meeting that he would look unfavorably upon any division manager who didn't cooperate in the effort. Yet, some lower level managers and supervisors insisted customers required the circuitous, confusing, and redundant text and that the command media improvement team couldn't touch the wording. Auditors, they said, would punish the organization. In the other case, the organization would be violating legal commitments, said a team member.

In both examples, pockets of functional management argued that, without great detail in the manuals, employees would violate company rules and circumvent established administrative processes. They might even contract for services outside the company if the manual didn't provide information about some internal services.

For all of these reasons, and to establish a consistent standard for achieving nimbleness, the litmus test was introduced—the foundation of a zero-based approach to streamlining documentation.

The litmus test works well in both large and small companies. It begins by assuming an organization needs no documentation—that's the zero—and adds a document only if it passes a test. The litmus test is based on the premise that documentation band-aids, for example, procedures or bulletins issued to resolve an audit crisis, are long-term resource drains. Once included in a manual or other medium, documentation band-aids seem to stay there forever. Everyone is afraid to touch them, and their maintenance is costly. There is a better way.

With the zero-based approach, companies typically avoid the justification mode, where departments or individuals argue to keep procedures that support their existence or play into the "that's the way we've always done it" syndrome or act as document hypochondriacs afflicted with audit band-aids disease. It is far easier to streamline procedures if an organization starts with a clean slate. For organizations that have no procedures (such as new businesses), the zero-based approach is a good way to avoid growing a future document maintenance burden.

A zero-based approach, rather than arguing for *excluding* a given document or portion of one, requires the document's owners to justify its *inclusion*.

Request concrete evidence, such as an ISO 9001 clause that specifies a procedure on quality records. The not-so-fine distinction is the difference between deleting existing documentation versus starting with nothing and demanding proof to add anything. It is the difference between a lengthy process that may result in minor wording compromises versus a sleek schedule whose major victory is an agile, easy-to-use world-class manual.

Rather than deciding which existing documents or parts could be sacrificed, streamlining teams for the two organizations assumed no document was needed and added one only if it passed the litmus test.

The litmus test consists of four questions. A positive answer to any one of the questions justifies inclusion—or at least further study—of a document or part. Four no's and the document, or part of it, is history:

1. Is it required by law?

2. Is it specified by contract?

3. Is it necessary for prudent business operations?

4. Would any harm come to the organization if the document, or part of it, was eliminated?

Let's look at some examples for each litmus test question.

1. *Is it required by law?* A city ordinance that prohibits smoking at a company's facility may require employers to state that regulation in an administrative procedure. A state law may specify conspicuously posted notices of its workers' compensation appeals process. U.S. federal law may specify the number of years required to maintain financial records. International legal agreements may outline export documentation requirements.

> **Checklist 2.1:**
> **Litmus Test**
>
> ☐ Is it required by law?
>
> ☐ Is it specified by contract?
>
> ☐ Is it necessary for prudent business operations?
>
> ☐ Would any harm come to the organization if the document, or part of it, was eliminated?

Teams responsible for streamlining an organization's documentation should ask to see a copy of the applicable law or regulation. Anything less will pile up documentation quickly to pre-improvement levels.

2. *Is it specified by contract?* Many contracts or purchase orders are vague in defining documentation requirements, yet an organization's internal functions often will interpret them narrowly. For example, a contract may read simply, "Seller shall maintain documentation." Yet a quality assurance manager, subscribing to the more-is-better theory of documentation, tells a streamlining team not only what kind of documentation is required by the contract, but also how long the contract states it must be kept! The manager

may truly believe there is more to read between the lines. Some people don't realize, or realize later, that unnecessary documentation is a noose by which an organization can hang itself. If the contract doesn't specify more documentation, and no other litmus test question warrants a positive answer, don't add more to your system.

3. *Is it necessary for prudent business operations?* What are prudent business operations? This litmus test component is a bit harder to interpret. What is prudent to an accounts receivable supervisor may be superfluous to a production project manager. What's prudent to a programmer may be inadequate to a buyer. There is no easy answer to all situations, but defining business needs clearly and supporting them with evidence can help.

For example, keeping specified records according to the ISO 9000 series of quality standards is required to maintain ISO certification. For companies registered to one of the ISO 9000 series standards and wishing to be recertified to meet marketing objectives, maintaining the records would be justified as a prudent business practice. Other examples of prudent business practices include complying with Baldrige Award criteria, the ISO 14001 standard for environmental management systems, Food and Drug Administration (FDA) regulations, and any other documentation required for quality, the environment, safety or purity, or other standard to which an organization is certified or at least with which it complies.

In all cases, it is wise to ask to see the business case or the requirements of the standard to apply this litmus test component.

4. *Would any harm come to the organization if the document, or part of it, was eliminated?* The last question is a safety net. Some documentation requirements are less tangible than laws, contracts, or standards. For example, a utility company may target a campaign to sway public opinion toward increasing rates. Without an increase, the company may no longer be fiscally healthy. If reducing the number of mailers sent to customers is seen to hurt the company's chances for passing an increase, then the answer to question four would have to be "yes." We rarely think of media mailers when we think of documentation, but don't they share some of the same resource requirements as procedures manuals or records? Doesn't someone in the organization, or a subcontractor, write, edit, and publish each mailer, keep files on each, process returned mailers, and so on?

Harm can come to an organization if it promises documentation to a customer and doesn't deliver. It can be harmful if the absence of expected documentation frustrates employees and reduces productive work time. An organization can be harmed if lack of documentation causes employees to make errors or perform redundant tasks.

How do you test for harm without harming? You do what a jury of peers does. You ask for reasonable evidence.

All the best efforts at streamlining an organization's documentation during an improvement initiative may be lost and the situation could worsen if the zero-based approach is abandoned during subsequent documentation reviews or if reviews never happen and documentation is added at will. *Every* time someone wants to add documentation—whether it is a new policy, a sentence to an existing procedure, a copy to a file, a mailer, an on-line form—the originator or another designated party should subject the addition to the litmus test. Otherwise, documentation will put on weight again. This time, people will be less enthusiastic to remedy the problem. They will say, "We've been there, done that." Educate employees, especially managers, about the costs of cumbersome documentation. Teach them to use the litmus test routinely and build in responsibility for containing documentation. It is that important.

Before using any precious resources to write or revise a document, ask if it is even needed. Whether evaluating existing procedures to eliminate redundancy and improve access or determining whether a new form should be developed, establish decision-making criteria. The litmus test fills that role well.

C. Streamlining: A Case Study

It is one thing to specify the components of Nimble Documentation® and to define a need-oriented, zero-based system and a powerful decision tool, the litmus test, for achieving Nimble Documentation®. It is quite another, however, to redesign, develop, and implement a streamlined system from existing documentation.

Every organization will use different steps and follow a different schedule to streamline its existing documentation system. Organization culture, size, condition of current system, process complexity, number and type of product or service lines, regulatory jurisdiction, industry, employee skills, resources, and many other factors affect a streamlining path. However, one successful effort can guide another organization to attain its own streamlining objectives. This section presents a case study of The Aerospace Corporation's achievement in streamlining its corporate policies and practices. It shows how a team serving more than 3000 employees integrated many COE characteristics with a zero-based documentation approach (see also Chapter 9). Other sections of this book present aspects of a similar streamlining effort accomplished at Hughes Aircraft Company (see Chapter 5).

Background

In 1995, The Aerospace Corporation began a corporate policies and practices streamlining effort that was based on its 1990 activities to reduce document volume and coordination cycle time and the recommendations of a more recent process improvement team. The Corporation planned an integrated policies and practices function to

- Meet contractual, legal, and prudent business requirements
- Reduce expenses
- Reduce processing cycle time
- Improve customer satisfaction
- Establish processes and metrics for continuous improvement
- Assume leadership in streamlining corporate policies and practices and in making them more accessible to users.

A corporate team working with an external consultant was created to streamline manuals and recommend steps toward establishing a comprehensive COE and sustained continuous improvement.

A Team with Three Goals

The manager of corporate memory resources, who was experienced in records management, led the team initially and was succeeded by the manager of the corporate directives department. The quality assurance office assigned a team facilitator. Team members represented major administrative functions and included the Corporation's Washington, D.C. office. The manager of HR and administration and the corporate communications manager sponsored the team.

The improvement implementation team identified three goals, each represented by a schedule track.

- Track 1. Revise, rework, and improve Corporate Policies and Practices.
- Track 2. Improve electronic access.

- Track 3. Achieve other process improvements, including document coordination and revalidation.

Activities

The team's major activities are listed here according to the following headings: project management; hierarchy, structure, and format; data and metrics; and electronic access. Figure 2.4 is a chronology drafted prior to the start of the documentation improvement project. Its usefulness lies in its comprehensiveness. Not all activities were implemented at The Aerospace Corporation; however, other organizations may benefit from considering the range of possibilities presented here.

Project management. The consultant met with the team's leader and participated in weekly, and later, biweekly team meetings and occasional meetings with team sponsors and corporate executives. The consultant also led the Track 2 meetings for several months, until the computing services department assigned a leader, and also collaborated on implementing project management activities with the team leader and facilitator, which included the following:

- Establish team members' responsibilities.

- Assign a monitor from each function.

- Schedule project activities.

- Communicate with and gain commitment of executive managers.

- Publicize and promote the streamlining initiative through company publications and giveaways.

- Develop the kickoff presentation.

- Prepare metrics of baseline and improved processes.

- Research other companies' documentation systems and processes (benchmarking).

- Brief Corporation business directors.

Checklist 2.2: Producing Zero-Based Documentation (A Streamlining Effort)

☐ Determine the need.

☐ Identify all readers, including their language requirements.

☐ Review existing documentation.

☐ Review processes.

☐ Perform a gap analysis between needed documentation and existing documentation.

☐ Determine signatory.

☐ Identify, select, or develop hierarchy, structure, and format.

☐ Establish document protection.

☐ Establish backup and retention provisions.

☐ Establish metrics for continuous improvement.

☐ Adopt writing style.

Once a team (or an individual) determines the need for a document or a group of documents, how do the team members proceed? What are the steps? Although each organization's customers and unique requirements will determine the steps and sequence, the general approach outlined here has worked well for The Aerospace Corporation and for many other organizations. Repeat steps in the process as needed, for example, additional revisions after reviews. Also consider document-template software. It doesn't replace the hardest part, capturing an organization's own processes in writing (or graphics or video), but it can be a starting point. Be careful, however. The temptation is strong to adopt a template (or borrow another organization's documents) without customizing it thoroughly. You may end up with terminology unfamiliar to employees and a style incompatible with the organization's culture. You may end up with someone else's procedures! And auditors and examiners, rightly, will not accept that. Worse, your organization will miss the benefits solid documentation affords and may incur liability. The following steps are useful to develop a Nimble Documentation® system from scratch or to improve an existing system.

1. Determine the need (for example, customers' requirements, regulations, laws, business goals, and quality standards or awards).

2. Identify all readers, including their language requirements.

3. Review existing documentation.

4. Review processes.

5. Perform a gap analysis between needed documentation and existing documentation.

6. Determine signatory.

7. Identify, select, or develop document hierarchy, structure, and format.

8. Establish document protection.

9. Establish backup and retention provisions.

10. Establish metrics for continuous improvement.

11. Adopt writing style.

12. Format draft according to processes and responsibilities.

13. Review draft (for example, by subject matter owners, related functions).

14. Revise draft.

15. Proofread revised document.

16. Submit revised document for approval.

17. Publish documents, either hard copy or electronically.

18. Notify users.

Figure 2.4. Producing zero-based documentation.

- Prepare a request for automated computing services.
- Negotiate the computing services department's commitment and resources.
- Lead Track 2 subteam meetings.
- Propose archiving and remote storage considerations.
- Establish a schedule for revalidating streamlined Policies and Practices.

☐ Format draft according to processes and responsibilities.

☐ Review draft.

☐ Revise draft.

☐ Proofread revised document.

☐ Submit revised document for approval.

☐ Publish (hard copy or electronic).

☐ Notify users.

The concept of accessing an on-line system instead of hard copy manuals for Corporate Policies and Practices was new and not entirely palatable initially to some employees. To assist users in becoming more comfortable with the change, the team developed a publicity and promotion campaign that included articles in the Corporation newsletter and announcements in the employee events publication (see Figure 2.5).

NEW! IMPROVED!
POLICIES AND PRACTICES

Coming to a terminal near you!

Watch for leaner, more accessible Corporate Policies and Practices debuting on PCs beginning November.

Policies reduced from 89 to 12, Practices about half. Pages skinnied down. Simpler language, too. View the new Policies and Practices soon on the web and search with a powerful tool that quickly finds the information you need.

A Corporate team has been working in conjunction with CDEFG to transform the Policies and Practices into a strong but flexible foundation positioned for a dynamic Aerospace future. The new system will save time, dollars, paper, and employee frustration.

Watch for instructions soon, so you too can say "hello" to better working though technology!

Call [   ], team leader, ext. 12345, or [   ], manager, Corporate Directives, ext. 56789, for more information.

Figure 2.5. Announcement to publicize and promote the streamlining initiative.

The team distributed to each corporate function self-stick notepads (giveaways) printed with an image of a desktop computer, a goals statement, and words promoting clear, concise, and accessible documentation (see Figure 2.6). Employees would multiply the value of the giveaways each time they used a self-stick note to send internal correspondence. Also, the team distributed promotional tent cards and placed them on library and cafeteria tables. To maintain readers' interest, two versions of the tent cards were distributed at intervals, each with two different messages (see Figure 2.7). The giveaways and tent cards were printed on the same neon-colored paper of the cover sheets for distributing approval drafts of the newly streamlined policies and practices. The team's intent was to reinforce each publicity activity by projecting a coordinated image of the streamlining effort.

Hierarchy, structure, and format. The team reached consensus on proposing a hierarchy of directive documents and a consistent structure and format for Policies and Practices (see Table 2.2). The proposal was modified only slightly during implementation. For example, 12 policies were included instead of 13 policies. Recommendations noted procedures and work or desk instructions; however, the team deferred structure and format decisions for these lower-tier documents to functional teams that would be streamlining them later. The decision process included

• Define the hierarchy for the Corporation's directive documents.

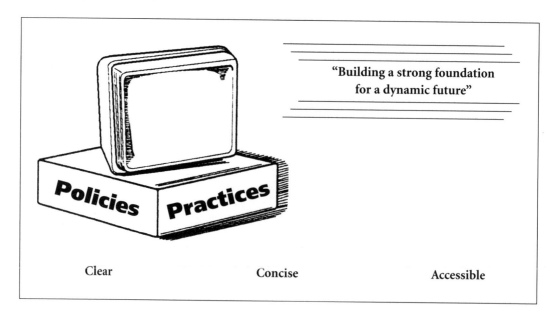

Figure 2.6. Self-stick notepad giveaways.

ON A DIET?
SO ARE THE CORPORATE POLICIES &
PRACTICES

LOOK FOR THE LEANER, STREAMLINED P&Ps
DEBUTING SOON

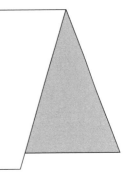

SAY "GOOD BYE" TO PAPER CUTS & PAGE
FUMBLING

JOIN THE ELECTRONIC AGE!

INSTANT ACCESS TO CORPORATE POLICIES &
PRACTICES

ON-LINE BEGINNING OCTOBER 30

READY - FOR EASY ACCESS TO CORPORATE POLICIES &
PRACTICES?

SET - FOR LEANER P&Ps WITH A NEW LOOK?

GO! - ON-LINE BEGINNING OCTOBER 30

P   olicies and Practices are being redesigned

&   soon will be accessible, easily, on-line.

P   repare to be excited with our new and leaner look

s   oon an electronic version will replace that great big book!

Figure 2.7. Promotional tent cards.

Table 2.2. Proposed directives hierarchy, structure, and format.

	Policies	Practices	Procedures
Number of documents	12	tbd	tbd
Number of books	1: Policies & Practices combined	1: Policies & Practices combined	tbd
Defined	Position of the Corporation	Implement Policies: (What is done)	How-to's: Implement Practices (Let people know the established way to do work)
Responsibilities section	Delete	Include if RESPONSIBILI-TIES format (see **Other sections,** below). Otherwise omit this section and embed responsibilities in PROCESS section	Functions decide
Definitions section	Delete	Include only if needed to clarify	Functions decide
References section	Delete	Delete	Functions decide
Other sections	Goal: 1 section without section heading	• GENERAL • PROCESS or • RESPONSIBILITIES (but not *both* PROCESS & RESPONSIBILITIES)	Functions decide
Signatory	Level 6 or 7	Level 4 or 5	Head of function
Document number system	Maintain basic system	Maintain basic system	Future consideration: Flow down from Policies & Practices: Same number + distinct suffix (e.g., HR 2-40-2.1)
Paragraph number system	Maintain basic system	Maintain basic system	Maintain basic system if it works for procedures
Signature authority information	Delete	tbd	tbd
Date format	Slashes vs. dashes	Slashes vs. dashes	Functions decide

- Establish a structure for the Policies and Practices manual.
- Establish the format of Policies and Practices.
- Design a flow-down document-group numbering system.
- Establish a document numbering scheme.
- Establish signature authorization levels for directive documents.

Prior to the documentation improvement initiative, some of the same information appeared in the separate Policies manual and Practices manual. After defining the function of Policies, Practices, and Procedures, the streamlining effort yielded one manual housing both the slimmed down dozen or so Policies, and the Practices reduced by half. Document reviewers deleted the *Responsibilities* section in the Policies and also in the Practices when a *Process* section included information about responsibilities. Definitions were pulled out of Policies and were made optional for Practices. In other words, they were included only when critical to understanding the Practice, such as for special usage of a term. Because the next track of the improvement initiative was to establish an on-line system for Policies and Practices, where users could search easily across documents, the *References* section was deleted from both Policies and Practices.

Data and metrics. The corporate directives department began working toward combining its S&P analysts' individual databases for processing documents (including coordinating their review, editing, and publishing) into a standard, departmentwide database, which would include document status (for example, *in coordination* or *approved*), number of pages, and other metrics. This activity was to be completed after the Corporation accomplished the primary streamlining effort. Major data and metrics proposed for the streamlining initiative included a cost model for processing and maintaining Policies and Practices; document volume; currentness; cycle time; zero-defects quality, including standards and measurement; page hits for users of the intranet system; zero-based approach to documentation; and editorial guidelines, such as simplified language and reduced verbiage. The team established and maintained volume and currentness metrics during the initiative, and S&P analysts became more skilled at editing for clarity and conciseness, however, baseline and regular measurement of these data were to be developed. The team largely adopted the zero-based approach to documentation. The electronic hits metric, which will allow the corporate directives staff and document owners to monitor the frequency with which users view Policies and Practices, was being developed. Other metrics—cost model data, cycle time, and zero-defects quality—were to be developed. The following improvements were accomplished.

• Volume (number of documents and pages). In January 1995, 90 Policies and 218 Practices constituted the two-volume Corporate Policies and Practices manual. As of January 1997, 131 streamlined Policies and Practices were published and about 33–36 additional Practices were in work. The decrease from 308 documents to 168 or fewer was a reduction of at least 45 percent. Individual Policies and Practices were streamlined as well; the combined page count was 1094 prior to April 1995, and in January 1997 was 315 pages, which is expected to increase to about 390–400 with publication of the documents in work—a reduction of at least 63 percent. Further, text clarity and reading ease increased considerably as a result of new editing standards.

• Currentness. Before the initiative, about 62 percent of Policies and Practices were from 1–5 years old, 17 percent were published in the last 6–10 years, 9 percent were 11–15 years old, and about 1 percent were older than 15 years.

With the publication of the in-work 33–36 Practices, none of the documents will be older than two years. This accomplishment is particularly significant because of the Corporation's substantial recent organizational changes; an accelerating rate of change both within the Corporation and specific to the aerospace industry; and rapidly changing HR, environmental, and other regulations affecting all organizations in the region and in the industry. Reviewing Policies and Practices regularly and revising them accordingly were never more important. Streamlining the documentation system and individual Policies and Practices allowed the Corporation to do that faster.

Electronic access. The streamlining team's leadership and the Corporation's computing services organization collaborated with the consultant to design, develop, and implement the on-line storage and retrieval system. Except for closed areas, nearly all of The Aerospace Corporation's employees are able to access and easily search the Policies and Practices and other corporate information on the Corporation's intranet. The pages (screens) were designed in .html format and the streamlined Policies and

Practices were published on the web. "What a relief to not have to hoist multi-pound volumes about and search for some elusive detail in a Policy!" said Dr. George Paulikas, executive vice president, in a congratulatory e-mail message to the team.

During the first few months of the new system, both old and new Policies and Practices were available in separate on-line databases. A special screen allows users to identify at a glance the documents that have been added, revised, or canceled during a moving window of 12 weeks. That way, users who haven't accessed the system because of vacation, travel, or other reasons, can learn the changes that have been made during their absence.

The team secured internal training for users. For example, Netscape training was conducted that included instruction on using Verity's TOPIC search engine.

Hard copy distribution was virtually phased out, but the corporate directives department maintains signed, hard copy masters and history files of all Policies and Practices.

The team planned to install a terminal in the library to allow employees to access the on-line documentation. It also was working on alternatives for closed areas and Track 3 activities, primarily electronic coordination (reviews) of draft Policies and Practices.

The on-line system was designed, developed, and implemented through the following activities:

- Define attributes of a people-friendly, easy-to-search on-line system.

- Eliminate hard copy manuals (retaining masters and a handful of hard copies for critical areas that have limited or no access to the on-line system).

- Present the proposed on-line system to the Corporation's computer user group.

- Define the Track 2 schedule.

- Draft the initial design of on-line system menus.

- Provide central area access to the on-line system.

- Coordinate document format troubleshooting (some applications needed initial modification).

- Coordinate development of user instructions.

- Coordinate uploader training.

- Develop alternatives for closed areas.

- Establish hotline support.

- Propose passive e-mail notification of document additions, revisions, and cancellations.

- Develop training alternatives.

Additional recommendations. At press time, the Corporation was considering additional recommendations for continuing to grow a documentation COE. Primarily, suggestions fell into six areas: database, metrics, cost, proactive role in electronic access, writing standards, and standard operating procedures.

1. *Database.* Establish a single database of Policies and Practices, including key process dates, page numbers, coordination status, and disposition. Off-the-shelf software will automate data generation, saving analysts time and increasing data accuracy.

2. *Metrics.* Provide charts regularly (for example, monthly or quarterly) of key metrics such as volume, proofreading, processing cycle time, customer satisfaction, intranet page hits, and possibly other data that will help COE staff continue to improve processes. Map activities and identify value-added and non–value-added tasks. Consider eliminating or reengineering non–value-added tasks.

3. *Cost.* Knowing the cost of each major process helps COEs make the best decisions about their processes. For example, if a requester submits a new draft Practice, the COE estimates the cost of producing and maintaining the document and persuades organizations to reconsider a request, especially if the document is only marginally useful. It is hard to run a business well without knowing how much it costs to do business. It is worth spending some time initially to gather cost data. See the cost model in Chapter 5 for a way to measure documentation processing costs.

4. *Proactive role in electronic access.* COE personnel, in addition to an organization's computing services organization, are proactive in helping employees use the new on-line system for Policies and Practices. COE staff participate in cascade training. That is, the staff is trained in locating and searching documents on the electronic system and then, in turn, train other employees.

The COE staff members maintain a database of help requests directed to them to pinpoint areas where more publicity or training is needed and where the system might need some adjustment to make it easier for employees to use.

5. *Writing standards.* To achieve consistency in writing and editing (which aids readers) and save time resolving editorial issues, the COE adopts a writing style guide—for example, *The Chicago Manual of Style* (University of Chicago Press, 1993) or one of many others—and a departmental writing convention guide that is specific to the organization and its documentation.

6. *Standard operating procedures.* The next recommended step in streamlining The Aerospace Corporation's directive documentation is to review standard operating procedures that apply to internal functions. Each procedures manual "owner" is responsible for this effort.

The following general course of action is suggested.

- Establish the flow down from Corporate Practices to existing operating procedures.
- Review each procedure using the same litmus test criteria: Retain procedures required by law, contract, or prudent business and eliminate those whose absence would cause no harm to the Corporation.
- Note any new required procedures.
- Establish structure, format, and editorial guidelines and develop coordination and revalidation processes.
- Establish all relevant metrics for continuous improvement.
- Revise needed procedures and disposition the remainder.
- Publish procedures on the same on-line system as the Policies and Practices.
- Publicize the new procedures and train users.

Convene a single team of procedures manual owners to establish a renovation process (tailored to the needs of each function), then have each participant work through the initiative with his or her staff and report status regularly.

Figure 2.8 shows the preliminary schedule for implementing documentation improvement at The Aerospace Corporation. It is a useful model for other organizations.

Model Schedule for Implementing Documentation Improvement:

Where Do We Go From Here

Notes: Assume team members are responsible for all activities unless otherwise noted. Assume team modifies the chronology according to its own information and expectations.

Track 1: Revise, Rework, Improve Policies and Practices

1A: Foundation—Facts and Data (weeks 1–4)

1. Develop cost model for gathering data.

2. Determine basic metrics for existing Policies and Practices including

   • Cost

   • Processing cycle time (number of days)

   • Currentness (percent last reviewed within team's standard, for example, 36 months)

   • Volume (number of documents)

3. Corporate Directives graphs baseline basic metrics and maintains the information monthly.

4. Pilot one section of the manual to determine an estimate of basic metrics for reengineered Policies and Practices. Use the criteria of legal, contractual, and prudent business practice. Assume zero-based documentation.

5. Estimate target basic metrics for reengineered Policies and Practices and implementation costs.

6. Refine team goals to include estimated variances in metrics.

1B: Commitment (weeks 5–8)

7. Present the data and goals (see 1A: Foundation) to Group executives and directors one-on-one and to their staff meetings. Request their commitment for zero-based documentation and resources.

8. Consult with executive managers regarding minimum requirements for regional offices.

9. Meet with function heads and signatories for each section of the manual. Request their commitment for zero-based documentation and resources.

10. Present the data and goals to the customer. Request the customer's support.

11. Present the data and goals to bargaining unit leaders. Request their support.

12. Publicize commitments and support. Use quotations wherever possible (for example, in the Corporation newsletter).

1C: Manual and Document Structure (weeks 2–10)

13. Review, then decide on a hierarchy of directives. Define each type of directive to be maintained in the system.

Figure 2.8. Preliminary documentation improvement implementation schedule.

14. Decide on the basic content and target number of Policies. (Include Regional Office members in all Policies decisions.)

15. Determine format for the Policies.

16. Identify the disposition for each existing Policy (whether it will remain, become a Practice, be consolidated with other Policies, or be canceled).

17. Ask the managers to identify representatives for each function to participate in one or two highly structured focus group meetings to determine a Practices format. The representatives also will lead the work team group for actual streamlining of Practices. Consider eliminating facsimile forms (if they exist) from Practices.

18. Propose a structure for regional offices Practices (for example, Policies only, Policies with matrix flow down). Consult with Regional Office heads to plan implementation of Regional Offices manual, if it is different from headquarters.

19. Personally and by memo invite each identified functional area representative. Send a copy to their immediate supervisor. Include the agenda in the memo, especially the original team's recommendations for any elements to eliminate or revise (such as Purpose or References).

20. Convene the focus group. Reach a consensus on format.

21. Consult with each functional area, and determine which (if any) portion and extent of Practices to decentralize (such as analysis, coordination, text processing, or the entire process). Review Team 1 (earlier team) survey data to identify Practices where employees might desire more detailed information (such as HR).

22. Corporate Directives recommends a writing style guide and standard text processing software, considering compatibility with candidates for electronic text retrieval system. It presents its recommendations to the team and receives the team's approval.

1D: Content (weeks 7–25)

23. Determine the participants for each functional area's work team, in conjunction with the identified work team leader. Assign a Corporate Directives analyst as a consultant to each work team (on call).

24. Supply the work teams with the Practice format, writing style guide, and text processing standards. Work teams adopt zero-based documentation criteria. Negotiate target dates for submitting drafts of Practices or other disposition decisions to Corporate Directives (consolidating, moving to lower-level directive, canceling, or streamlining). Require monthly status reports from each work team to be submitted to Corporate Directives, Directives Team to include metrics on the number and percent of Practices accomplished and remaining to be reviewed, dispositioned, redrafted, and so forth. Present monthly status (metrics) to function heads. Work teams complete and submit drafts.

25. Corporate Directives edits drafts and prepares them for signatories.

Figure 2.8. *Continued.*

26. Corporate Directives publishes the new manual, either by sections or in its entirety, and provides an audit trail matrix. Another alternative is to publish the manual on an electronic retrieval system, preempting publication of the new manual. Still another alternative is to distribute limited copies of the new manual pending imminent conversion to an electronic retrieval system.

Track 2: Improve Electronic Access (sketch of a few proposed activities—weeks 2–?)

27. Consult with information systems specialists and Team 1 survey results to develop criteria for rating off-the-shelf client-server electronic information retrieval packages. Be sure to include purchase, licensing, and maintenance costs. A small sample of other features includes

    • Adequate number of users possible simultaneously

    • Balancing sophisticated searching with extensive training requirements; generally, the more precise the search capabilities, the more training needed

    • Response capabilities, such as the ability to request org charts from on-line screens

28. Research off-the-shelf packages according to identified criteria. Review literature and benchmark or benchtrend with other large companies (what works for 30 users won't necessarily work well for 3000).

29. Participate in demonstrations of off-the-shelf packages.

30. Tentatively identify the package that best meets the organization's criteria.

31. Pilot the package with a portion of the revised Policies and Practices.

32. Estimate the time to reach a break-even point for implementing the electronic retrieval system. Plan to maintain two systems simultaneously during the toddler months of the electronic system.

33. Gain commitment for budget and HR for conversion investment (see methods in Track 1). Seek applications for the system outside of Corporate Policies and Practices (such as cafeteria menus, rideshare information, credit union rates, internal job opportunities, and clubs). Plan to upload approved organizational announcements and urgent information bulletins immediately, even during the phase of redundant systems (hard copy and electronic). These applications will help speed acceptance of the conversion and will help employees become familiar with the system.

34. Sponsor a conversion implementation team.

35. The conversion implementation team determines elements and timeline. Examples of critical elements include

    • Standard naming and menu conventions

    • Screen identification, such as manual name, document name, and screen number of total screens

Figure 2.8. *Continued.*

- Closed area considerations and alternatives
- Just-in-time printing
- E-mail notification
- Centralized versus decentralized uploading
- Conversion date and notification schedule for canceling all but emergency hard copy manuals. (Recommend four to six months notification with regular notification updates.)
- Publicity campaign for conversion
- User and information provider training schedule
- Central access to system, such as the library or cafeteria terminals
- History files, offsite storage (disaster recovery considerations)
- Electronic coordination
- Accommodate lower-level (how to) directives

36. Establish and implement information provider maintenance, such as menu revision.
37. Publicize the electronic information retrieval system.
38. Train users and information providers.
39. Develop hotline support during and following the conversion. The hotline function maintains user metrics to identify problems and consider modifications, publicity, and training.
40. Develop or apply a system feature to measure use, such as the number and type of directives hits.

Track 3: Achieve Other Process Improvements (weeks tbd)

41. Streamline coordination process. Consider electronic coordination.
42. The team or Corporate Directives establishes a revalidation process requiring approval, revision, or cancellation of Practices (x-year cycle). Revalidation metrics established, maintained, and publicized monthly (activity in Phase 1).

Figure 2.8. *Continued.*

PART II

Implementation

CHAPTER 3

Hierarchy, Structure, Format, and Style

Solutions presented in this chapter address documentation challenges such as

- A useful hierarchy for company documentation
- When to use a plain vanilla text format for procedures
- When to use alternative formats such as play script, process map, or video
- The critical elements of a procedure
- When to use passive and when to use active sentences
- How to avoid "dog puppies" for concise writing

This chapter introduces the *Implementation* topic group of this book. Once an organization commits to streamlining its existing documentation or creating a nimble system from scratch, it must define the vehicles for fulfilling the need. The way the system and its parts are organized and presented (that is, its hierarchy and structure, and the format and style of documents) should facilitate access to and comprehension of needed information.

For the purposes of this book, *hierarchy* is the relationship of manuals, or other groups of documents, to each other. For example, quality policies may be the broadest or highest level of direction on processes and responsibilities that affect the quality of an organization's products or services. These policies may be implemented by standard operating procedures—the how-to's—which are the next level. Finally, work instructions, detailed direction for each job, flow down from the procedures. *Structure* is the way documents are organized to form a manual or other group of individual documents, such as procedures. The internal organization of an individual document is its *format,* for example, what sections of a procedure are included, such as Purpose, Process, and References, and how they are presented, such as plain vanilla text, play script, or process map. Finally, *style* is at the level of paragraphs, sentences, phrases, words, and mechanics.

From a practical hierarchy compliant with ISO 9000 standards to a compact structure for corporate policies and practices to a format for a multilingual workforce to a style that speeds forms processing, this chapter provides practical guidance for implementing a world-class documentation system.

A. Hierarchy and Structure

Defining a common hierarchy of management and operating documentation is especially important in large companies, but it is needed by organizations of every size. Most often, we see policies, practices, procedures, instructions, and specifications. Good information access and traceability dictates that higher level documents flow down clearly and logically to lower level ones. Also, quality initiatives, such as the ISO 9000 series, require an outline of documentation used in an organization's quality system. For example, ANSI/ASQC Q9001-1994 clause 4.2.1 states

> *The supplier shall prepare a quality manual covering the requirements of this American National Standard. The quality manual shall include or make reference to the quality-system procedures and outline the structure of the documentation used in the quality system. (American Society for Quality Control Standards Committee for American National Standards Committee Z-1 on Quality Assurance 1994)*

Draft an enabling directive document (policy, practice, or procedure) that defines your organization's document management program, including the purpose and format of each type of document. This may be the first practice (or policy or procedure) in the series.

The hierarchy of quality system documentation shown in Table 3.1 is useful for meeting ISO 9000 series and the requirements of other quality initiatives.

Table 3.1. Hierarchy of quality system documentation.

Component	Description
Quality system manual	Highest level directive documentation (quality policies)
Operating procedures	What processes shall be performed by what function
Work instructions	Step-by-step direction on how to perform processes
Job descriptions	Responsibilities for assignments or positions
Records	Evidence of events and results
Forms	Information templates
Data	Facts, information, and statistics

It would be hard to imagine a nimble quality system manual longer than 30 pages. No more than 20 is better. However, the quality system manual will be longer if operating procedures are also housed in it. Three examples of operating procedures are supplier qualification, inspection and testing, and training. Work instruction topics include data entry, designing fulfillment packages, and purchasing coordination. Job descriptions include quality assurance manager, HR coordinator, and receptionist. Payment histories and subscriber inquiries are records. Forms, both electronic and hard copy, include purchase requisition and consultant confidentiality statement. An example of data is software-driven instructions for generating mailings.

It is prudent, and required by law, to maintain internal controls for transactions, for example, to commit company funds. However, the less bureaucratic the approval authority system, the better it is for everyone. Rather than specifying in a practice or procedure who has authority to sign for what, maintain a separate chart of approvals. That way, when individuals change positions, the practices and procedures that mention the individual's authority will not have to be revised—and writers won't have to search through all the practices and procedures for the employee's name. To further reduce maintenance, list approval authority by function rather than by employee's name. See Chapter 8 for more on approval authority systems.

Bulletins, memos, or announcements convey urgent or temporary information. They can be holding places for a practice or procedure being written. Establishing expiration dates is a good idea for bulletins; otherwise they have a way of piling up and are challenging to maintain or access. Seasonal information or reminders lend themselves well to temporary bulletins, such as company policy on holiday decorations and accepting gifts from vendors.

Table 3.2 shows a basic hierarchy that is useful for management and operating directive document systems for the largest companies, those with several sites and divisions; both The Aerospace Corporation and Hughes Aircraft Company have adopted hierarchies like this one. Smaller firms, however, having complex processes or serving highly regulated industries, might consider a similar structure.

Both Hughes Aircraft Company and The Aerospace Corporation streamlined their top level policies to about a dozen one-page documents; in the first case, from about 75 policies, and in the second from 89. In neither organization did the streamlined policies lose essential information. For companies with more than 500 employees, policies covering the functions shown in Figure 3.1 and perhaps a couple of additional ones to meet an organization's special needs are useful. A single policy statement may be adequate for smaller companies.

Figure 3.2 is an example of a streamlined policy. It communicates the company position on business operations. Note its broad terms and brevity.

Not every level is needed for every company. The fewer levels, the better. A company with a single product line and simple processes may be able to assemble a single-volume manual that includes the firm's quality policy and quality management system and procedures relating to the quality of its product. Work instructions, rather than being included in a manual, may be posted in transparent sleeves above corresponding machinery. Cross-functional work and flexible positions may nullify the usefulness of static job descriptions; posted work instructions may capture needed direction adequately.

Table 3.2. Basic hierarchy for corporate documentation.

Component	Description
Policy	Position of the company
Practice	Description of processes and responsibilities Implements policy
Procedure	Detail of process and responsibility Implements practice
Desk or work instruction	Step-by-step performance of a job
Form	Information template
Signature approval system	Authorization to commit funds or other resources Implements forms transactions
Bulletin	Temporary or urgent direction for any level of specificity

1. Human Resources

2. General Management (or Administration)

3. Property or Material (or Purchasing)

4. Legal (or Contracts)

5. Finance

6. Facilities

7. Information Resources (including public information and computers or automation)

8. Ethics

9. Safety and Health

10. Security

11. Quality Assurance

Figure 3.1. Useful policies.

A consistent, integrated document numbering scheme supporting broad to narrow information helps users place documents within an overall hierarchy and facilitates access to other documents with broader and narrower scopes. For example, a company's HR policy is numbered HR-4. A practice covering the company's career development system is identified as HR-4-2. A procedure for applying for a job transfer is HR-4-2-3, and the application is company form 4-2-3A. The approval authority system indicates employees authorized to approve transfers via form 4-2-3A. Such a numbering scheme helps users find all of the information they need to handle the transfer process.

Tables of Contents and Indexes

A table of contents section in a hard copy manual is important for maintaining change notices and revisions to the manual. The most useful tables have space to write in document revisions and additions and their issue dates. Documents are alphabetized by title and include issue dates. Cover sheets for distributing documents explicitly instruct users to update their table of contents when filing new or revised documents or deleting obsolete or canceled ones. An updated table should be distributed at intervals corresponding to the frequency of revisions, additions, and cancellations. Semiannual and quarterly distribution schedules are common. The revision date is printed on

---

THE GHI	
COMPANY	**POLICY**

		NUMBER:	BUO-1
SUBJECT:	**Business Operations**	DATE:	May 13, 1995
		PAGE:	1 OF 1

The Company conducts business prudently. It exercises and effectively communicates adequate controls to manage its operations and commitment to promote and safeguard its assets.

The President and Chief Executive is authorized to approve and delegate all internal actions and external commitments required for business operations according to (1) the chart of approvals and (2) management directives disseminated by Policies, Practices, Bulletins, Internal Procedures, Organization Charts, and Organizational Announcements.

Management communicates complete and timely information regarding federal, state, and local government action that could affect the Company and informs government authorities of the characteristics, needs, and interests of the Company.

As a good citizen of the community, the Company informs the public of its activities and participates in community affairs to promote a better understanding of the Company and its mission. To protect its assets, including its positive public image, the Company registers original and distinctive names, logos, marks, publications, and other items with agencies of the federal government and establishes guidelines for their use.

We C. Policy, Sr.
President and CEO

Figure 3.2. Example of a streamlined company policy.

the table itself, along with information identifying the manual. Figure 3.3 shows a brief table of contents for a new company just beginning to develop its documentation system; the document numbers correspond to major clauses of ISO 9001 standards.

The key to locating information in hard copy manuals is a comprehensive index with generous cross references. Not all employees look up information using the same words that writers think they will. Prepare an index with many synonyms. (See Chapter 7 for more on indexes in user manuals.) Take advantage of the index feature of major word processing programs. But

[XYZ LOGO]		Operating Procedures

Contents

	Number:	AAAP TOC
	Date Issued:	00/00/96
	Page:	1 of 1

AAAP Number	Title	Date Issued
1-2-1	Chart of Approvals	8/7/96
1-2-2	Employee Suggestion Program	8/7/96
2-3	Continuous Measured Improvement (CMI) Plan	8/7/96
4-0	Design Control and Configuration Management System	8/7/96
4-1	New Product Brief Development	8/19/96
5-0	Directive Document System	8/19/96
5-2	Forms Management System	8/21/96
6-0	Vendor Qualification	8/23/96
6-1	Vendor Certification	8/23/96
14-0	Corrective Action	9/9/96
18-0	Training	9/9/96

Figure 3.3. Sample hard copy procedures manual table of contents.

keep in mind that an index is a maintenance-intensive part of documentation. Every time a document is revised it is an obligation to review all index entries related to the document. Publish a revised hard copy index according to the frequency and extent of document revisions. Semiannual or quarterly indexes are common. However, more and more organizations are moving to on-line document storage and retrieval systems to facilitate information access. Part of the appeal (and savings) of cutting-edge on-line systems is their automated indexing capabilities and powerful search engines. Some systems can search not only for synonyms but also for more general and also narrower terms. Many can be used for context-dependent searches. For example, users interested in documents related to software engineering might not want to retrieve documents associated with an organization's Software Engineering Division.

B. Format

Documents are vehicles for communicating information. They are successful to the extent they do that according to customers' requirements. In Chapter 2, five sources of need were identified (and probably there are many more), which included users as internal customers and external customers. How do you format a document to meet a customer's requirements?

To illustrate format alternatives, their relative advantages and disadvantages, and their elements, let us look at standard operating procedures, a common vehicle for communication and the common denominator of most organizations' documentation systems. Considerations for formatting procedures, however, work well for other documents. Individual format elements, such as scope or responsibilities paragraphs, differ for policies, practices, user's guides, forms, bulletins, organization charts, and so on. And because companies vary in their culture, history, and receptivity to new approaches, several alternatives are illustrated. Selecting an option should be based on the organization's and its customers' needs and readiness.

Variations within each format include indentations, if any; heading style and contents; graphic emphasis, such as lines and boxes; and many others. The possibilities are nearly endless. Following this section, important elements of a procedure are discussed, no matter the format or variation.

Advantages and Disadvantages of Several Document Formats

Formats for standard operating procedures, and a practice, include variations of

- Plain vanilla text (or narrative)
- Play script
- Modular
- Flowchart
- Process map
- Video
- Audio

Headers in the following examples vary but are not necessarily tied to the particular format illustrated. Headers can include the company logo, document type (operating procedure), title, document number, revision letter and date issued, signatory, page of total number of pages, and a separation bar.

Plain vanilla text (or narrative). Essentially, the plain vanilla text format presents paragraphs with a few headings (see Figure 3.4). Paragraphs may be indented or not, headings may be numerous or few, and numbering can be applied to major sections only or every paragraph (or something in between). More or less, this is the traditional format seen often in manufacturing and design firms. To demonstrate this format's versatility, a second version of the plain vanilla text format is shown in Figure 3.5; this one has a spare numbering scheme. A third example of the plain vanilla text shows a practice format (see Figure 3.6).

> *Advantages*
>
> *The plain vanilla text format conserves paper by fitting many words on each page. It meets traditional expectations and looks like what many people think a procedure should look like. Typically, auditors are familiar with this format. Numbering sections to the third digit (Figure 3.4) helps users communicate, for example, when a user calls out a paragraph. Numbering to this extent also helps viewers if conversion is made to an on-line system. The numbering scheme of the second version of this format (Figure 3.5) is aesthetically more pleasing. The practice numbering scheme (Figure 3.6) is simple and easy to read. Also, for many writers, plain vanilla text is easier to write than other formats.*
>
> *Disadvantages*
>
> *The narrative format takes longer than others to locate information. It does not reflect energy or project a dynamic image. Numbering to the third digit (Figure 3.4) is cumbersome to read.*

Play script. The play script format is action oriented. A popular version of this format includes two sections: scope and procedure. The procedure section is divided into responsibilities and actions. Responsibilities, which are listed on the left, are numberless. Action paragraphs, typically, are numbered simply with uppercase letters and Arabic numerals. Numbering schemes for the play script format vary. Figure 3.7 is the XYZ engineering company's procedure in a play script format.

> *Advantages*
>
> *The play script format facilitates finding information for which each function is responsible. White space is friendly to readers. This format reflects more energy than the plain vanilla text and projects a more dynamic image.*

[XYZ LOGO]   **Operating Procedure**
                    Receiving Inspection

Number:	**XYZP 4-2**
Date Issued:	**Rev. A**
	May 5, 1996
Page:	**1 of 1**

1.0   SCOPE

Applies only to shipments received at the Buffalo plant from outside suppliers.

2.0   PROCEDURE

2.1   Field Installation (Site)

2.1.1   Inventories and marks up the shipper within 24 hours of arrival.

2.1.2   Dispositions any discrepancies between shipping's copy of the shipper and installation's copy of the shipper as follows.

   A. Site supervisor contacts shipping lead.

   B. Lead determines availability of the discrepant material.

   C. If discrepancy remains unresolved, site supervisor calls Installation (Buffalo) and issues a field request for missing items.

   D. If site has parts not identified on the shipper, field installation office calls shipping and resolves discrepancy.

2.1.3   Faxes the marked up shipper to Buffalo field installation office c/o the installation coordinator.

2.2   Installation (Support Coordinator)

2.2.1   Forwards faxed copy of shipper to planning.

2.3   Planning (Clerk)

2.3.1   Clerk matches and attaches the faxed copy of the shipper to the planning copy of the shipper and files them together.

   Note: Planning's copy should be filed only with field installation's copy.

Figure 3.4. Example A of plain vanilla (or narrative) procedure format.

[XYZ LOGO]

Operating Procedure

Receiving Inspection

Number:	XYZP 4-2
Date Issued:	Rev. A
	May 5, 1996
Page:	1 of 1

1.0   SCOPE

Applies only to shipments received at the Buffalo plant from outside suppliers.

2.0   PROCEDURE

Field Installation (Site)

    A. Inventories and marks up the shipper within 24 hours of arrival.

    B. Dispositions any discrepancies between shipping's copy of the shipper and installation's copy of the shipper as follows.

        1. Site supervisor contacts shipping lead.

        2. Lead determines availability of the discrepant material.

        3. If discrepancy remains unresolved, site supervisor calls Installation (Buffalo) and issues a field request for missing items.

        4. If site has parts not identified on the shipper, field installation office calls shipping and resolves discrepancy.

    C. Faxes the marked up shipper to Buffalo field installation office c/o the installation coordinator.

Installation (Support Coordinator)

Forwards faxed copy of shipper to planning.

Planning (Clerk)

Clerk matches and attaches the faxed copy of the shipper to the planning copy of the shipper and files them together.

    Note: Planning's copy should be filed only with field installation's copy.

Figure 3.5. Example B of plain vanilla (or narrative) procedure format.

| THE EFG | |
| COMPANY | # PRACTICE |

		NUMBER:	6-70-21
SUBJECT:	**Contact with Outside Auditors**	DATE:	5/14/96
		PAGE:	1 OF 2
		SUPERSEDES:	(Same)
		DATED:	10/7/95

GENERAL

The Internal Audit Department represents the Company in all contacts with external auditors concerning audits of Company activities, in accordance with Company Policy 6-70.

RESPONSIBILITY AND PROCESS

1. Internal Organizations

   a. Contact and refer to the Internal Audit Department when contacted by an external auditor or asked formally for information.

   b. Contact the Contracts Directorate regarding audit visits arranged through the LMN Contracting Officer.

   c. Contact the Internal Audit Department to request audits of subcontractors prior to purchasing goods or services.

2. Internal Audit Department

   a. Appraises, coordinates, and monitors external audits of Company activities.

   b. Advises line management on all issues related to external audits.

   c. Assists external auditors in meeting their objectives, including compiling and transmitting requested information.

   d. Communicates information and coordinates correspondence about each audit directly to cognizant management.

   e. Approves, coordinates, and transmits formal replies to requesters.

   f. Reviews and approves audit replies prepared by other organizations.

Figure 3.6. Example C of plain vanilla (or narrative) practice format.

THE EFG COMPANY	PRACTICE

		NUMBER:	6-70-21
SUBJECT:	**Contact with Outside Auditors**	DATE:	5/14/96
		PAGE:	2 OF 2
		SUPERSEDES:	(Same)
		DATED:	10/7/95

3. Contracts Directorate

   a. Performs services outlined in paragraphs 2.b. and 2.c. applicable to audit-related visits arranged through the LMN Contracting Officer.

   b. Maintains a central file of all information pertinent to auditor activities.

C. D. Practice
Executive Vice President

Figure 3.6. *Continued.*

[XYZ LOGO]	**Operating Procedure**	

Receiving Inspection

	Number:	XYZP 4-2
	Date Issued:	Rev. A
		May 5, 1996
	Page:	1 of 1

1.0   SCOPE

Applies only to shipments received at the Buffalo plant from outside suppliers.

2.0   PROCEDURE

Responsibility	**Action**
Field Installation (Site)	1. Inventories and marks up the shipper within 24 hours of arrival.
	2. Dispositions any discrepancies between shipping's copy of the shipper and installation's copy of the shipper as follows.
	A. Site supervisor contacts shipping lead.
	B. Lead determines availability of the discrepant material.
	C. If discrepancy remains unresolved, site supervisor calls Installation (Buffalo) and issues a field request for missing items.
	D. If site has parts not identified on the shipper, field installation office calls shipping and resolves discrepancy.
	3. Faxes the marked up shipper to Buffalo field installation office c/o the installation coordinator.
Installation (Support Coordinator)	1. Forwards faxed copy of shipper to planning.
Planning (Clerk)	1. Clerk matches and attaches the faxed copy of the shipper to the planning copy of the shipper and files them together.

Note: Planning's copy should be filed only with field installation's copy.

Figure 3.7. Example of play script procedure format.

Disadvantages

The play script format consumes more paper—if hard copy—or more screens—if electronic—than other formats. Its numbering scheme can be confusing because several paragraphs are assigned the same number. This format is nontraditional, therefore some employees may need training and time to adjust to it. Also, writing in the play script format is more difficult for many writers than other formats.

Modular. The modular format works well with fairly straightforward, step-by-step procedures and especially with those that have *if-then* decision points. Parts of the procedure, or modules, are self-contained. Usually, a separate modular procedure is required for each function or process. The first modular format example for the XYZ engineering company applies to the field installation function only (see Figure 3.8). Module numbers are kept to a minimum. Then, for contrast, Figure 3.9 shows a nonstructured text procedure (plain vanilla text format minus the section headings and indentations) and Figure 3.10 shows Raymond Urgo's structured/modular format for backing up information on a PC.

Advantages

Modular formats facilitate finding information. Their partitioned, graphic layout is easy to follow. If-then decision points are set off; they do not interfere with the procedure's flow. Minimum numbering is unlikely to distract readers. Modular formats project a contemporary image often associated with software user manuals and other high-tech products.

Disadvantages

Modular formats consume more paper—if hard copy—or more screens—if electronic—than structured (divided into sections, paragraphs numbered) plain vanilla text. Procedures designed to this format usually take longer to develop. Like the play script, modular formats are nontraditional. Some employees may need training and time to adjust to them. For many writers, the modular format is the most difficult text format.

Flowchart. A procedure structured as a flowchart relies largely on graphics to convey information. This format also is often used as a step between the process interview for generating a procedure and a written draft. Documentation

[XYZ LOGO]	**Operating Procedure**
Title: RECEIVING INSPECTION	Page 1 of 2
Number: XYZP 4-2	Approved By: Quality Manager
Revision: A	Date Issued: May 5, 1996

Reason   Consistent quality of purchased material

Scope   Applies only to shipments received at the Buffalo plant from outside suppliers.

Responsibility   Field Installation

Procedure

1. INVENTORY and MARK UP the shipper within 24 hours of arrival.

2. RESOLVE discrepancies between shipping's copy of the shipper and installation's copy of the shipper, as follows:

If shipping's copy of the shipper **agrees** with installation's copy of the shipper—	—MOVE material to staging platform.
If shipping's copy of the shipper **disagrees** with installation's copy of the shipper—	—Site supervisor: • CONTACT shipping lead and describe discrepancy. —Lead: • DETERMINE availability of discrepant material.
If discrepancy is **resolved**—	—MOVE material to staging platform.
If discrepancy is **unresolved**—	—Site supervisor: • CALL installation's office (Buffalo). • ISSUE field request for missing items.

Figure 3.8. Example of modular procedure format.

[XYZ LOGO]	**Operating Procedure**
Title: RECEIVING INSPECTION	Page 2 of 2
Number: XYZP 4-2	Approved By: Quality Manager
Revision: A	Date Issued: May 5, 1996

If parts **identified** on the shipper—	—MOVE material to staging platform.
If parts **not identified** on the shipper—	—Site supervisor: • CALL shipping and resolve discrepancy.

3. **FAX marked up shipper to Buffalo field installation office c/o installation coordinator.**

Figure 3.8. *Continued.*

BACKING UP YOUR FILES ON A PERSONAL COMPUTER

It is imperative to make frequent backups of your files to safeguard and preserve your data. If a file is deleted for some reason, the only way to recover its data is from a backup copy. You should back up your files on a scheduled basis. Also, back up the files when they are new or when the information is highly critical.

The number of diskettes you will need for the backup depends on how much data are in a file. (A 3.5-inch diskette holds 1.44 megabytes.) Backup diskettes must be formatted ahead of time because formatting does not occur during the backup process.

From the File Menu of the word processing program, highlight the name of the file to be backed up. From the Edit Menu, select the option BACK UP. A pop-up window will inform you to insert a diskette. At this point, insert a diskette into the drive and press ENTER to continue. If a pop-up window says the backup is completed, exit the Edit Menu. If the window says the backup is incomplete because there is insufficient space, replace the diskette with another formatted diskette then press ENTER to continue the backup.

Always remember to remove the diskette. It may be helpful to place a label on the diskette and write the name of the file on the label.

There are two sources of information in the event that you need more information on backing up your file. One is the user guide for the word processing software. The other is the PC Workstation Support Group.

Source: Raymond E. Urgo, handout at presentation to Orange Empire section of American Society for Quality Control, 1995. Used with permission.

Figure 3.9. Example of nonstructured and nonmodular plain vanilla text format.

teams use flowcharts routinely to see a process without text distraction. Flowcharts help individuals spot non–value-added activities and needlessly cumbersome processes. For some employees, flowcharts are foreign and intimidating, but most see them as helpful tools.

Flowchart steps are depicted by standard geometric shapes. The flowchart format shows processes and direction at a glance, including easy-to-spot decision points. It is often used as a preliminary step in drafting a procedure in a more traditional, written format. Many organizations tape a huge sheet of paper to the wall and draw a master flowchart of their functions in preparation for writing traditional procedures.

An S&P improvement team at Hughes Aircraft Company drew a flowchart to illustrate the process for canceling Group practices (GSPs). In the diagram, shown in Figure 3.11, the team had just begun electronic coordination of GSP drafts using a customized version of Digital Equipment Corporation's (DEC) Videotex system (GSGDOC). Major input for the cancellation was requested

How to Back Up Files on the Personal Computer

Importance

It is important to back up files to safeguard and preserve your data. If a file is deleted or the hard drive fails, the backup copy is the only way that you can recover the lost information.

When to back up files

It is best to back up your files on a scheduled basis, especially when a file is new or the information is highly critical.

Before you begin

Before you begin a backup, you must have a sufficient number of formatted diskettes. (One 3.5-inch diskette holds 1.44 megabytes.)

Procedure

From your word processing program, follow these steps to back up your file.

Step	Action
1	Open the File Menu.
2	Highlight the name of the file to be backed up.
3	Open the Edit Menu.
4	Select the option BACK UP.
5	Insert a formatted diskette into the drive.
6	Press the ENTER key for the backup to occur.
7	Wait until a message appears. | IF this message appears . . .	THEN . . .
---	---
Backup completed	• Go to Step 8.
Backup not completed—insufficient space	• Remove the diskette. • Insert another formatted diskette. • Repeat Steps 6 and 7.	
8	Exit the Edit Menu.
9	Remove the diskette.

For further information

For further information, either
• Refer to the word processing software user guide, or
• Contact your PC Workstation Support Group.

Source: Raymond E. Urgo, handout at presentation to Orange Empire section of American Society for Quality Control, 1995. Used with permission.

Figure 3.10. Example of structured modular format.

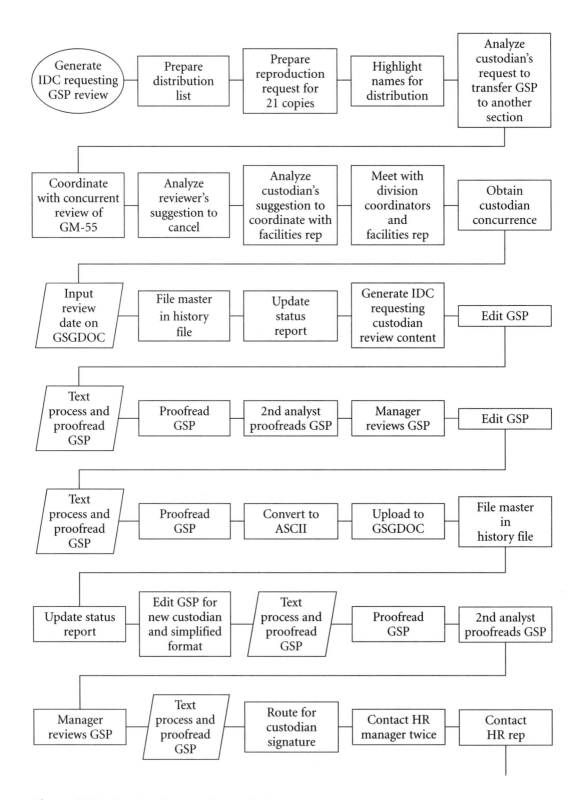

Figure 3.11. Flowchart for canceling an obsolete practice.

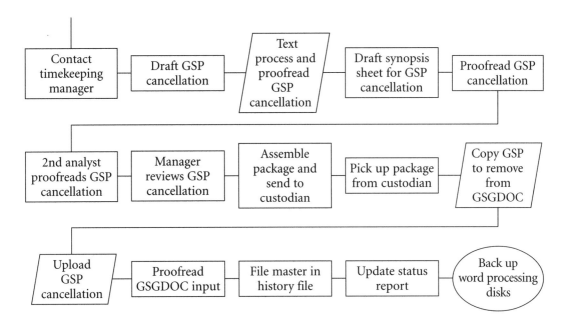

Figure 3.11. *Continued.*

rom timekeeping and HR functions. The IDC referred to in the chart is the ompany's name for an internal memorandum (interdepartmental correspon- ence). The custodian was the document owner who had the authority to pprove the cancellation. At the time the chart was drawn, ownership of the ocument was between two functions: timekeeping and HR. Note that this owcharting activity contributed to finding a better way to streamline docu- entation, which stimulated the creation of zero-based documentation.

Advantages

A flowchart's graphic representation, for most people, is easy to follow. If-then *decision points draw the reader in quickly because of their distinctive shape. The flowchart format, because it contains few words, usually is easier to understand by users who may be less than proficient in the language of the procedure. This format projects a contemporary image often associated with software development and other high-tech processes.*

Disadvantages

The flowchart format takes longer to develop with conventional word processing software. (Flowcharting software is readily available but may not be standard in a company.) Procedures written in the flowchart format are still nontraditional for many companies (but are becoming more popular, especially with quality assurance organizations and process improvement teams). Some employees may need training and time to adjust to it. Procedures written in the flowchart format may not lend themselves well to text-based importing and exporting activities.

Process map. The flowchart format modified to include additional dimensions, such as multiple functions and decision points, becomes a process map. If a process is cross functional, maps are an especially useful tool for improving it. Process maps accomplish two major objectives: They document primary steps in a process, and they show the relationship between functions involved in a process. In improvement efforts, teams use process maps to analyze the way a process currently is being accomplished, develop a better way, and then implement the changes. As a procedure format, the process map documents primary steps in a process and shows the relationship between responsibilities or functions involved in the steps. Process maps graph movement and direction. Teams use the process map format as a preliminary step in writing a traditional procedure, especially if more than one function is involved. An example of a process map for processing a document is presented in Figure 3.12. Groups involved in the process are listed on the left. On the right are rectangles that show process activities and ovals depicting measurement points.

Advantages
The process map graphic format, like the flowchart's, is easier for many people to follow than written procedures, especially if proficiency is limited in the primary language of the documentation. Process maps can show cross-functional responsibilities at a glance. Procedures represented in process map format show activities occurring simultaneously.

Disadvantages
Like the flowchart format, the process map's takes longer to develop with conventional word processing software. (Also, process mapping software is becoming more available but may not be standard in a company.) Procedures written in the process map format are nontraditional (but, like the flowchart format, are becoming popular with quality assurance organizations and process improvement teams). Most employees need

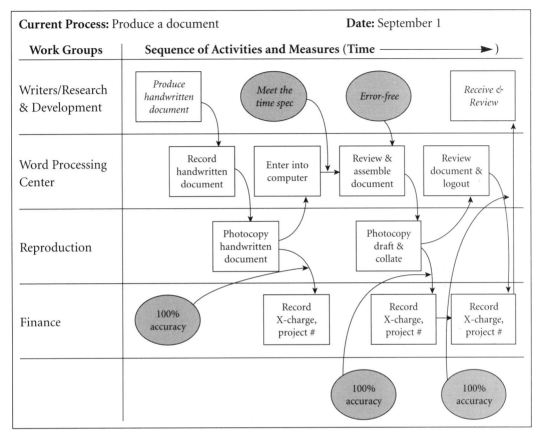

Current Process: Produce a document   **Date:** September 1

| Work Groups | Sequence of Activities and Measures (Time ⟶) |

Figure contents:

Writers/Research & Development: Produce handwritten document; Meet the time spec; Error-free; Receive & Review

Word Processing Center: Record handwritten document; Enter into computer; Review & assemble document; Review document & logout

Reproduction: Photocopy handwritten document; Photocopy draft & collate

Finance: 100% accuracy; Record X-charge, project #; Record X-charge, project #; Record X-charge, project #

100% accuracy; 100% accuracy

Source: The Rummler-Brache Group, *Cross-Functional Process Flow,* 1987. Adapted and used with permission.

Figure 3.12. Process map example.

training and time to adjust to the process map format. Procedures written as process maps may be difficult to import and export with text-based software.

Video. Organizations are beginning to use video formats for their procedures. Video clips are getting easier to include in computer-delivered documentation. Video is an acceptable alternative to written procedures for meeting quality and industry standards, such as the ISO 9000 series.

Advantages
Video is useful for showing a technical process in detail and for a multilingual workforce. Sophisticated videos can illustrate several processes or functions simultaneously. Employees are used to

viewing monitors, like televisions, and generally find videos more appealing than written or graphic documents.

Disadvantages
Videos are costly to produce, compared with other procedure formats, and are costly to update as processes change. Equipment for showing videos may not be readily available at all sites where procedures are needed in an organization. It may be time-consuming to access just a small piece of information at a time. Not all auditors accept videos yet in lieu of more traditional procedure formats.

Audio. A few organizations take advantage of the benefits of spoken procedures, either on tape, compact disk (CD), or from a computer system.

Advantages
An audio format makes sense for visually impaired employees. It is also useful for sighted employees who have limited reading skills or for those who wish to learn a process while driving or in other alternative settings.

Disadvantages
Formats other than audio generally are more useful for locating small segments of information quickly (however, segmented audio clips in computer software promise to be more commonplace). Audio recorded procedures may be costly to update.

Table 3.3 summarizes major considerations for selecting the procedure formats just described.

Format Elements
Few topics related to documentation attract as much controversy as the elements to include in a document. Some insist that all procedures should have a purpose statement. Others see this element as redundant.

Going back to the basics of Nimble Documentation®, the zero-based approach is extended to format elements. In Chapter 2, the litmus test was presented for deciding whether to include a document. This customer-based test asks if the document is required by law, contract, or prudent business practice, including quality and industry standards, and whether the organization will be harmed if the document were not there. Applying the test to

Table 3.3. Considerations for selecting procedure formats.

Considerations	Procedure Formats						
	Plain vanilla text	Play script	Modular	Flowchart	Process map	Video	Audio
Time-consuming or costly to produce			X	X	X	X	X
Graphic				X	X	X	
Written language reliant	X	X	X				
Special training needed			X	X	X		
Dynamic				X	X	X	
Shows multiple functions at glance					X	X	
High-tech look				X	X	X	
Paper and screen thrifty	X						
Good prelim to written				X	X		
Easy to find info		X	X		X		
Shows decision points				X	X		
Good for text-based import and export	X	X	X				
Good for visually impaired							X
Good for hearing impaired	X	X	X	X	X	X	

format elements, ask: Is the element required by law, contract, or prudent business? Will the organization be harmed if the element were omitted?

Try the litmus test with one of the most controversial elements, the purpose statement, which is found at the top of plain vanilla text, play script, and other formats for policies, practices, procedures, work instructions, and other documents. Does any law require a purpose statement? Does a contract require it? What about prudent business? Can you think of any standard that specifies a statement of purpose? Is there anyone who can prove his or her organization will be hurt if a procedure goes without a purpose statement? Few purpose statements pass the litmus test. An alternative is to strengthen the title so the document's purpose is clear. Banish statements like

---

PURPOSE: The purpose of this procedure is to establish a procedure to . . . .

Review other documentation for similar statements. Instead of beginning a memorandum with, "The purpose of this memo is to . . . ." write a clear, but concise, subject line. Tell the purpose of a letter directly, without telling your readers, "The purpose of this letter is to . . . ." If the purpose of your document is unclear on its own, rewrite it so it is clear.

When an organization establishes a system for the first time or embarks upon a major documentation overhaul, a fine opportunity emerges to assemble document owners, usually representatives of functional areas, and ask them what elements they need. Hold a focus group meeting and challenge participants to show why they need a purpose statement or any other element. Hughes Ground Systems Group did that and, along with other streamlining actions, cut the page count of written practices in about half. Keeping out unneeded document elements allows readers to locate information faster, reduces processing and maintenance time, and lowers expenses.

Other document elements that are candidates for the litmus test follow, along with considerations for their inclusion.

- Organization name
- Logo
- Document-group title

- Document title
- Document number
- Date issued
- Revision letter or number
- Page number
- Sections
- Related documents
- Numbering scheme
- Forms
- Definitions
- Signatory

Organization name. Readers expect the company or division name to be at the top of a document. That is where readers are likely to look first. Headers that include the organization name on every page help readers distinguish a document source, which is especially useful with suppliers, customers, or partners; or parent, sibling, or offspring organizations, for example, General Motors (or Raytheon), Hughes Electronics, and Hughes Aircraft Company subsidiaries. The most nimble on-line systems are capable of heading print-outs with the company or division name. Printed pages have a way of getting separated; an organization name on each page aids in their identification.

Logo. The decision to include a logo—preferably in the header, where people usually expect it to be—is based upon several factors. One is the importance of quick identification. Is a document likely to be mixed with others from other organizations, for example, a purchase order or letter? Another is the organization image. Will a logo-graced newsletter help market a school district department's services? Will a logo-topped quality policy help corporate divisions blend after a consolidation or merger? Consider omitting the logo or using a simpler one if it slows web site viewing or becomes scrambled on mainframe documentation systems.

Document-group title. A corporate policies and practices manual is a document group. Naming the manual, again preferably in the header, helps distinguish the document's source in the same way as the organization name. Although this element becomes less important as organizations use electronic information and storage systems, which can be searched across manuals, world-class systems name document groups on every printed or printable page.

Document title. The same considerations apply to memoranda and e-mail subject lines as to directive document titles. Include a title that covers the scope of the document, yet is concise. Save readers' time thumbing or scrolling through the wrong documents. Preclude the need for a purpose statement. A memo inviting employees to a meeting that will address vacation policies should be introduced by a subject line something like

---

SUBJECT: Meeting to Address Vacation Policies

In very busy offices, including the meeting date in the subject line might be even better for catching the attention of readers so they will put the meeting on their schedules, for example

---

SUBJECT: Meeting 9/15/98 to Address Vacation Policies

A too-general subject line is likely to fall to the bottom of a paper pile or e-mail in-box, such as

---

SUBJECT: Administrative Meeting

Document number. Many document number schemes are serviceable. The handiest correspond to quality or industry standards. For example, a distributor of plastic tubing adopted a document number scheme for its work instructions according to the ISO 9000 series. The work instruction for "Buyer" is numbered 4.6, akin to ISO 9001's section 4.6, Purchasing. A credit reporting service uses Form 4.14 for its "Correction Action Report," which corresponds to ISO 9001 section 4.14, Corrective and Preventive Action. The best document number system defines a clear flow down from higher level or broader documents. The same number stems are assigned to a policy, for example, and related practices or procedures, forms, and records (such as financial policy number FO-3 and procedure FOP-3.4). An integrated number scheme for an organization's entire documentation system facilitates information access and includes documents from policies to desk or work instructions to forms and records.

A minor consideration for document number is the number format. Before a documentation improvement initiative, one company division numbered its practices the same way it formatted the date on those practices: 09-04-03 and 09-04-96, respectively. The fact that these two numbers were immediately above one another in the header sometimes confused readers, if only for a moment. Fortunately, the division redesigned the date format to include slash rather than dash separators: 09/04/96. It was easier for readers than renumbering practices. Another option would be to spell out the date: September 4, 1996. Had the improvement initiative team retained the problematic date format, the new millennium could be expected to bring even more confusion!

Date issued. See the *Document number* section regarding possible confusion between a document number and the day it was issued. In many organizations, the date a document is published is not the same date it is signed. Does issue date mean the day the document appears on-line or the day its copies leave the mail room? Or does it represent the day the document owner approved it? Legal challenges have been raised regarding the date an HR policy was in effect and conflicting interpretations of the document's issue date. Avoid diverting your organization's resources needlessly. If an element is likely to be interpreted in more than one way, either revise the element (for example, change this one to *date published* or *effective date*), or define format elements in the system's enabling document.

Also, consider that traditional formats for dates vary among nations. For example, in the United States, MMDDYY (Month Day Year) is common, although DDMMYY is used sometimes. In Europe and Asia, however, DDMMYY is the traditional date format. Organizations doing business internationally should know that 3-12-97, for example, may mean March 12, 1997, in one country, but December 3, 1997, in another.

Revision letter or number. Revision letters or numbers on procedures, forms, and records may be a quick way to determine a document's version.

Some standards auditors insist on including revision letters or numbers. However, if the date is clear and there is no need to identify the document's original issue, a revision letter or number is redundant. It is an additional element to process and maintain.

Page number. To prevent separating document parts unintentionally or having recipients read just one side of a document that is printed back-to-back, include the statement *page X of X*. If another element clearly indicates the end of a one-pager, for example a closing or signature line, a page number is unnecessary.

Lengthy hard copy manuals that are revised frequently should be paginated by sections. That way, users can add or replace pages without reissuing the entire manual. One common numbering scheme is I-1, I-2, I-3 (for the first section), II-1, II-2, II-3 (for the second), and so on. Use a loose-leaf binder or another binding method that permits easy page insertion and removal.

Sections. What sections should be in a procedure? The answer depends on several factors. Include a *Scope* section only if some documents apply to only some employees or processes. Some organizations use the term *Applicability* or *Applies to* instead of *Scope*. Use a *General* section, and then another section below it, if some information in the document applies to all processes or functions under the title's umbrella (goes in the *General* section), but some information applies only to portions of it (goes in a subsequent section, for example, *Sampling separation*). Include *Policy* (or *Practice* or *Procedure*) and *Responsibilities* sections if they need to be distinguished from each other. Whatever you do, don't repeat information in both places. If the process is more important than who or what function performs it, use only a *Policy* (or *Practice* or *Procedure*) section. If the opposite is true, format the document according to *Responsibilities*, referring to processes in the context of the performing position or function. It is acceptable to have some documents in a manual follow a *Policy* format and others a *Responsibilities* format. Figure 3.13 shows an operating procedure formatted according to *Responsibilities*. Note a *Scope* section is included because the company has branches in other states where different procedures are followed.

Related documents. Documents accessible through an on-line information storage and retrieval system that has a powerful search engine do not need this section. It is a remnant of hard copy manual days. It is expensive to maintain and prone to audit problems. Every time a referenced document is

[Logo] ABC Company   Operating Procedure

Forms Management System

Number: ABCP 5-2

Date Issued: 08-07-96

Page: 1 of 2

1.0   SCOPE

Applies to business transactions between ABC Company (ABC) employees in Santa Ana and with ABC customers, co-marketers, vendors, and visitors.

2.0   RESPONSIBILITIES

2.1   Administration or Designee

A. Maintains a consistent forms management system to authorize, communicate, clarify, simplify, and control business transactions.

B. Assigns form numbers that correspond to ABC's quality system requirements.

C. Maintains and periodically distributes an index of ABC's current forms.

D. Reviews and coordinates new or revised forms to meet ABC's business goals, including improving the efficiency of information handling.

E. Reviews and coordinates requests to cancel obsolete forms or forms that no longer meet ABC's business goals.

F. Submits requests to Purchasing to print ABC forms used in large quantities.

G. Maintains stock of frequently used forms to meet user demand.

H. Maintains on ABC's LAN a master copy of each infrequently used form for employees to print as needed.

I. Maintains master copies and history files of ABC's forms.

J. Coordinates periodic reviews of forms for currentness and continuing need, and maintains records of the reviews.

Figure 3.13. ABC forms management system operating procedure.

[Logo] **ABC Company**   **Operating Procedure**

Forms Management System

Number:	ABCP 5-2
Date Issued:	08-07-96
Page:	2 of 2

2.2   Managers, Supervisors, or Designees

A. Originate new forms, or revisions, pertaining to business transactions involving functions under their responsibility.

B. Approve cancellation of obsolete forms or forms that no longer meet ABC's business goals.

2.3   Purchasing

Arranges printing of ABC forms used in large quantities.

_____
Wee R. Nimble, Chief Operations Officer

Figure 3.13. *Continued.*

added or deleted, all documents that refer to the addition or deletion need to be located and then updated. Viewers can search for a term across an on-line system and locate all related documents. However, where it is necessary to consult documents that may not be in the on-line system, for example, manufacturers' specifications or government regulations, a *Related documents* section could be essential. An organization may be able to delete this section even in a hard copy documentation system if the system's structure is especially clear and information overlap across documents is rare. Other terms for this section are *Applicable documents* and *Relevant documents.*

Numbering scheme. Numbering schemes for document groups were discussed in the Hierarchy and Structure section (A) of this chapter. Internal numbering, especially for directive documents, applies to document sections and paragraphs. Several factors contribute to the choice of numbering scheme, including communication ease, on-line versus hard copy system, and aesthetics. Documents that change frequently or are reviewed often by outside organizations may benefit from a scheme where every paragraph, subparagraph, and point is numbered. That makes it easier for employees, auditors, vendors, and others to communicate about individual paragraphs. In such situations and for the same reasons, bullets are discouraged. In a complex document, however, subparagraphs could push numbers to the fifth place or further, for example paragraph 6.1.2.2.3. The document then is cluttered with numbers and consumes a lot of paper or screens. It also looks uninviting. A compromise is to number to the second or third place, and then use letters, or to mix numbers and letters, including Roman numerals.

As already mentioned, numbers rather than bullets aid in communicating about particular document segments. For immediate impact, however, such as in marketing pieces or critical memos, bullets are preferred instead of numerals because bullets minimize the amount of discrete information presented to the reader. They "hit" the reader more quickly. Every numeral in a sequence is a new bit of information that readers have to process. It takes readers slightly longer to comprehend numbered items versus bulleted ones. On the other hand, every bulleted item, beginning the same, does not need the additional processing. For example

1. Plastic pouches are stored above the bench.

2. Metal ties are stored below the bench.

3. The Traveler is fastened to the front of the batch.

- Plastic pouches are stored above the bench.
- Metal ties are stored below the bench.
- The Traveler is fastened to the front of the batch.

On-line systems may pose a special challenge to document numbering schemes. Scrolling lengthy documents without plentiful paragraph numbers as guideposts can lose a user. For example, in the middle of a screen, a user sees paragraphs C and D. There is no indication what section or major paragraph the user is viewing. If the document were in hard copy, on the other hand, the reader could easily see several pages of it at the same time. Aesthetics may need to take a secondary role to users' convenience, and all paragraphs, subparagraphs, and points may need to be numbered.

However, to convey a breezier image, aesthetics may be placed above other considerations. For example, only major headings and paragraphs could be numbered in a work instruction that serves as a marketing piece for a desktop publishing firm. Leaving many headings and paragraphs unnumbered can present a less "procedurish" image.

Forms. Don't include copies of forms in policies, practices, procedures, work instructions, or any other directive document—period. And don't even consider generating a separate procedure for filling out a form. When a form changes, which happens often in growing, merging, or reengineering organizations, if a copy is incorporated in the document, the document becomes obsolete and must be updated. Refer to a form by name or number, not revision or date, in the body of the document. There is no need to list forms again in a *Forms* section. Users—people who fill out forms—should not have to open an on-line document or locate a hard copy manual to complete a form. Make the form clear so instructions are unnecessary; try a new form draft on people unfamiliar with the form's processes. Revise any unclear parts. If a form is necessarily complex, place instructions on the back of it. If it is computer-generated on demand and prints only on one side, include instructions on the face, but only for the potentially confusing parts.

Definitions. Some standards and regulations require that documents segregate definitions at the beginning or end of them for specified terms or words with special interpretations. More often, terms are assigned a definitions section by tradition. The best place to define a special term is in the body of a document, where the term is used, unless the term is used in many places in the document. That way, the reader does not have to flip pages or scroll to understand a process. The best way to define terms is with documents on an intranet system. In each document that requires a definition for a specific term, embed a link to the term's definition. That way, a reader who already understands the term won't be distracted, and a reader who doesn't can get the information quickly.

Signatory. To control documentation, which is a requirement of many specifications and standards, such as the ISO 9000 series, approval should be indicated by a hard copy signature or by an on-line printed name (approval line) backed up by a signature or password approved master. Organizations automating their documentation systems often fail to adopt a different set of considerations for their on-line systems. For example, a signature line at the bottom of a hard copy document may be appropriate. Readers can see at a glance the authority for the document. On-line, however, the signatory should be indicated at the top of a document. Readers should not have to scroll to the end, or press a quick key, to find out who authorized the document. To facilitate updating some documents without reissuing a manual, a signatory for each document is recommended over a single one for an entire manual.

Figure 3.14 is a list of the format elements just discussed. An asterisk precedes each one that is critical to a strong directive management program and especially to a quality initiative, such as the ISO 9000 series. *Not every listed element should be included in every directive document.*

C. Style

This book includes a discussion on writing style because style can make a huge difference in how well documentation achieves its goals. Few people look forward to reading wordy, circuitous procedures. Few enjoy shoveling to dig out important information in a bulletin.

Nimble Documentation® is not only more pleasant to read, it is also more effective. It saves time. It is more likely to be read, so people will be less likely to make mistakes, displease customers, or incur liability. Comprehensive guidance on helpful, rather than hurting, writing style is beyond the scope of this book; however, a few tips are offered in this section that can significantly improve the quality (read usefulness) of your documentation. The four areas are conversational rather than musty style, active versus passive voice, emphasis, and conciseness. Also addressed is a way to standardize your documentation to reduce time spent over resolving writing convention controversy.

```
*Organization name
 Logo
*Document-group title
*Document title
*Document number
*Date issued
 Revision letter or number
*Page number of total number of pages
 Sections:
        Scope
        General
        *Policy (or Practice or Procedure) or
        *Responsibilities
 Related documents
*Numbering scheme
 Forms
 Definitions
 Records
*Signatory
*Critical to strong directive management program and espe-
  cially to a quality system
```

Figure 3.14. Document format elements.

Use a conversational style. Avoid rubber-stamped phrases. This is a problem especially with bulletins, reports, and forms, but also with employee policies. Here are some examples of rubber-stamped phrases.

- Attached you will find, as per your request, two copies of the form.

- Regarding the matter and due to the fact that the plant closes . . .

- This is to advise you that submitted herewith is your notification of our compliance with subject standards.

- We deem it a great pleasure to approve your request as per memo of the 12th of August.

Rubber-stamped phrases are called that because little thought is given to what value they add to writing. Habit dictates their use. Take them out. Write instead

- We have attached two copies of the form.
- Attached are two copies of the form.

For the next ones, just state your message. Leave out the rubber stamps. For example

- The plant closes on . . . .
- We comply with subject standards. See attached . . . .
- We approve your request of August 12.

Write active. Nothing tightens up a document faster than converting passive sentences to active ones. Long, passive constructions wear out readers. Here are examples.

- Passive example: Corrective action is escalated by supervisors.
- Active example: Supervisors escalate corrective action.

Write active sentences when the information must be clear and direct and when it is important to identify responsibility. The active voice may be inappropriate if you wish to deemphasize the actor or emphasize the action. Switch to the passive voice when you want to hide the actor of your message, when the news is bad, when you want to be more tactful or soften the message, or when the action is more important than the actor.

> **Checklist 3.1:**
> **Nimble Writing Style**
> ☐ Write conversation-ally.
> ☐ Choose active versus passive voice according to goals.
> ☐ Emphasize.
> ☐ Be concise.

The subject of the sentence *performs* the action in the *active* voice. The subject *receives* the action in the *passive* voice. Here are a few examples.

Passive voice	Active voice
• A written evaluation will be made after six months of employment, which will be presented to the employee before a raise is recommended.	• The supervisor evaluates the employee's work in writing after six months of employment, then may recommend a raise.
• Initial figures for the bid were submitted before the June 1 deadline.	• The Engineering Department submitted initial figures for the bid on May 30.

Passive voice *(continued)*	**Active voice** *(continued)*
• When the quality plan is complete, it is to be rerouted for final approval.	• Reroute the completed quality plan for final approval.
• The raw data are submitted to Data Processing by the department rep each Friday.	• The department rep submits the raw data to Data Processing each Friday.

With passive writing, you can reach your destination, but the path won't be as smooth, will take longer, could cost more, and may get you hurt or lost (see Figure 3.15).

Emphasize. Use space (sometimes called *white space*)—generous margins, and space above, between, and below—to call attention to critical information, such as steps that readers historically overlook, and processes that, if not followed, result in waste or confusion.

Use mechanical means such as indentations, graphics, boxes, underscoring, boldface type, and italics to emphasize information. Too many kinds of emphasis in the document, however, confuses readers. Get over the novelty of your equipment's capability to use many colors or typefaces. Too much variety is distracting. Construct sentences and paragraphs to call attention to segments of writing. Position the most important piece of information either first or last. Use very short sentences to invite reading. But vary sentence length or the emphasis-intended sentences will lose their power to attract.

Be concise. Get out that hoe and weed your documentation. Use one or two simple words instead of a phrase and avoid *dog puppies* (redundancies), like the ones in Figure 3.16.

Before leaving document style, note that readability is also an important factor of style. Major word processing software includes measures of readability. However, many indexes are used, and the level they assign to sentences varies widely. Some readability indexes are based on number of syllables, others on sentence length, and still others on word novelty. Indexes also include more than one element. Rely on factors other than the indexes alone when estimating the readability of a document. For example, children as young as first graders rarely have difficulty recognizing the word *dinosaur,* because of their recreational experiences, such as movies, games, and coloring books. Yet, according to some readability indexes, *dinosaur* is higher than a 1.0 level word. Also, organizations often use multisyllabic technical words that are common either within the organization or its industry. A readability

Figure 3.15. The passive writing path.

a bolt of lightning	lightning
absolutely sure	sure
advance warning	warning
bad disaster	disaster
basic fundamentals	fundamentals
blend together	blend
blue in color	blue
consensus of opinion	consensus
continue on	continue
cooperate together	cooperate
during the course of	during
each and every	each OR every
end result	result
final conclusion	conclusion
first and foremost	first OR foremost
forever and ever	forever
kneel down	kneel
large in size	large
local residents	residents
major breakthrough	breakthrough
mix together	mix
new beginning	beginning
new innovations	innovations
new recruit	recruit
partially damaged	damaged
passing fad	fad
past history	history
qualified expert	expert
refer back	refer
square in shape	square
ultimate end	end

Source: Yvonne Lewis Day.

Figure 3.16. Dog puppies.

index might assign a high level to a sentence containing those words, but they won't be difficult for employees to read.

To avoid wasting time repeatedly on editorial conventions, such as whether to capitalize a recurring term, a documentation team should adopt a writing style guide and perhaps issue a brief guide tailored to any special editorial needs of the organization. The *Chicago Manual of Style* is one style guide. There are many others. Choose one that is comfortable and abide by it. Most organizations have a few writing conventions that, when violated, upset a few staff, such as spelling out executive titles or capitalizing the word *company.* Include known preferences to smooth the writing process.

CHAPTER 4

Electronic Alternatives

Solutions presented in this chapter address documentation challenges such as

- What are the benefits of standardization?
- Why use an intranet for document storage and retrieval?
- What features should be considered to establish an on-line documentation system?
- How can electronic imaging help and how can it hurt?

By far, the greatest gains in meeting customers' and other sources of needs and in reducing cycle time and costs of directive documents are in adopting an effective, standardized electronic processing, storage, and retrieval system. Preparing documents with word processing or desktop publishing programs and placing them on computers, even providing access to them through a LAN, is not the same thing.

Nimble Documentation® demands consistent processes to ensure reliable results, reduce processing time, and contain costs. When personnel performing the same function use the same processes (for example, tracking coordination of document reviews and uploading), they minimize opportunity for miscommunication and error. The rhythm of work continues uninterrupted if one person is absent. Further, as work load peaks and dips, standardization allows staff to perform understaffed functions temporarily. Automating processing facilitates standardization, and an electronic storage and retrieval system contributes to a consistent, trim, and cost-effective documentation system. However, processes should be automated only *after* zero-basing the documentation (see Chapter 2) and improving the processes to eliminate defects and rework; automating inefficient processes *first* would only increase the rate at which mistakes are made.

This chapter begins with a discussion of standardization, including references to a corporate documentation function that standardized its processing hardware and software. Then the chapter addresses major considerations for an automated document storage and retrieval system, including input, access, viewing, searching, printing, storage, logistics, and systems support. The chapter concludes with a discussion of electronic imaging.

A. Standardization

A documentation function typically realizes a fast return on investment when it standardizes computer hardware. The installation of new, standardized computers and peripherals, selected by a COE, is credited with maintaining one S&P department's productivity despite the retirement of several staff members. In the following case, standardization was so instrumental in process improvement that the positions left open by the retirees were withdrawn.

Under a reorganization plan, the S&P department of Hughes Ground Systems Group had consolidated several groups that handled documentation at the same facility. Several employees came from a manufacturing division, where they coordinated, edited, and published product operations procedures. Others came from one of the company's data processing organizations, where they maintained the information systems procedures manual. A property documentation function transferred in and so did the function that had handled configuration management procedures and engineering procedures. The department also included analysts who were responsible for a wide spectrum of practices and administrative bulletins, organizational announcements, organization charts and statements of responsibility, forms, and an approval authority system.

Checklist 4.1: Considerations for Standardization

- ☐ Meets needs
- ☐ Frequently used
- ☐ Saves time
- ☐ Reduces or eliminates errors or rework
- ☐ Designated by consensus
- ☐ Cost reasonable for results
- ☐ Training available
- ☐ Documented
- ☐ Accessible
- ☐ Reviewed regularly

Employees from some of the functions came with their PCs. Others brought their Macintosh computers. Some of the staff were trained to use, and happy with, MultiMate word processing software. Others knew WordPerfect best. Most used Microsoft Word. Even the communications software varied for using the LAN. Existing documentation that required revision was embedded with fonts that were compatible with some of the printers but made other ones stop. Some of the printers could be used only with some of the computers.

Facing yet another wave of staffing reductions compelled the department to find a more consistent way of doing business. A team investigated the feasibility and costs of standardizing the department's hardware and software. The team members interviewed each department staff member, found out his or her needs and experience, consulted with the MIS department, and issued recommendations. They considered their customers' software because other functions frequently sent rough drafts on disk to the department. The team weighed the anticipated learning curve for new equipment and software. They looked at the department's graphics needs. But more than anything, the team members saw the labor expense of continuing to work with incompatible equipment and mismatched software. Their findings justified replacing nonstandard hardware and software and obtaining staff training.

To avoid disrupting service to customers, the department planned a step-by-step conversion, enlisting the aid of MIS consultants when department expertise excluded some conversion steps. All department staff were trained before the switch was complete.

At another large company in Southern California, analysts who handled the company's policies and practices maintained two different databases for coordinating new documents and revisions. Each analyst took responsibility for different sections of the policies and practices manual and kept track of the process independently. One kept a computerized database; the other kept handwritten notes. When either analyst was unavailable, work in their sections halted. If a customer called, it was difficult to report document status.

Another way organizations can benefit from standardized documentation processes is to share macros and stylesheets for word processing. Experienced text processing specialists can establish shortcuts to formatting documents and post them on a networked server so anyone needing to assist can maintain the processes. Having several procedures writers adjust individual paragraph formats is a big time waster. Also, the auto text feature of popular word processing packages can be used to standardize frequently used terms, saving time and reducing error potential. Text processing personnel can use this feature especially for symbols, which often are time-consuming to retrieve and easy to mistype. Consistent use of macros and stylesheets can result in cycle time savings and fewer errors. The benefits of automating repetitive tasks are considerable—well worth the initial time and cost investment of advanced training.

Also, standard writing guides for documentation functions work wonders to maintain consistency and prevent needless controversy. Two guides are best: a published style manual and a list of organization-specific writing conventions.

Standardized processes and products have the greatest impact when

- They meet customers' requirements.
- The processes are used often.
- They return quality, cost, or cycle time benefits over their expense.
- Their intended users reach consensus.
- Staff are trained on their use.
- The standards are documented, accessible, and reviewed regularly for continued improvement.

B. Storage and Retrieval

Just a few years ago, an exciting system for document storage and retrieval allowed key word searches across manuals and up and down tiers. Today, internal, searchable electronic networks (intranets) speed document processing and access.

In the 1980s, Videotex by DEC could be customized to suit large documentation systems. Content owners specified key words for each document, up to a limit that increased with each software upgrade. Staff trained on mainframes uploaded documents. Users could access the system on many kinds of terminals and by modem from remote locations: dumb terminals, workstations, and desktop computers. Menus listed documents, but they could be selected only by commands. Soon, the command legends appearing at the bottom of the screen that once were seen as helpful became annoying to users, who now were becoming familiar with graphical user interface (GUI) computers, such as the point-and-click Macintoshes and then Windows and other operating systems.

The mainframe-hosted document storage and retrieval systems were a tremendous improvement over hard copy manuals. Documentation functions of many large companies were transformed. Users, reluctant at first to part with paper, began to feel comfortable with on-line searching. Both management and audit personnel were happier because nearly every employee had access to up-to-date manuals. Revised hard copy key word indexes, which consumed extensive resources to update, publish, and distribute, were obsolete even before they were delivered. With the on-line system, an updated index was accessible the same day a document was revised. Change notices no longer were necessary to publish and file. With minor programming, special menus could display all documents that were added, revised, and canceled over a recent, selected period of time, for example, 12 weeks—a boon for employees returning from travel or leave.

In the late 1980s, when Hughes Aircraft Company's Ground Systems Group S&P department introduced the Videotex on-line system for practices and bulletins, the cost savings, reduction in time to reach users, and other benefits were enormous (see Chapter 5). A catalog of company forms was added later, along with a response box to order hard copy organization charts (which, because the character size would be too small for legibility, were impractical to display on the system). Then, the approval authority system was automated; anyone could find out quickly who was authorized to approve company transactions. Higher level company policies became accessible, as did lower tier procedures and job descriptions. Soon training schedules, cafeteria menus, and other information was accessible.

All documents could be printed on either system or local printers or sent electronically to other users who had access. To maintain integrity of the current document version, the on-line system included a statement in an "enabling" practice—a document that defines the manual, including approval authority and maintenance responsibilities—that established that the on-line version prevailed, which is recommended for current on-line document storage and retrieval systems.

As more and more Hughes users obtained access to internal e-mail, features such as automatic notification were added to the system. Staff sent e-mail messages of document additions, revisions, and cancellations to users who requested them. Later, the coordination drafts were made accessible through Videotex, and reviewers were notified by e-mail when a document was available for their review.

Today's on-line document storage and retrieval systems have many additional features. Powerful search engines allow sophisticated searching. Personnel who upload documents no longer need to enter key words individually. Systems now support context-specific searches and searches by synonyms, broader terms, narrower terms, and other options. Commands are no longer required; users can access documents by pointing and clicking.

Intranets are now one of the most versatile vehicles for on-line documentation storage and retrieval systems. An Aerospace Corporation team streamlined its corporate policies and practices, then developed an intranet for storing and retrieving the documents. Users access information via Netscape, a popular browser, and Adobe Acrobat, which displays documents preserving formatting and graphics using portable document format (PDF). S&P personnel upload new or revised documents and archive canceled ones. Scripts written by corporate programmers automate menu changes. Because the policies and practices manuals were completely revamped prior to automating them, menus were specially designed to help users find information. Documents are listed several ways, including by ascending order of their former number, alphabetically by title, and according to their new number. Users can find documents also on 12-week screens (new, revised, and canceled documents). They can also search for information by entering a document number or title, or topic. The webmaster's e-mail link, posted at the bottom of each screen, gives users quick access to technical support.

An on-line system is an excellent medium for hosting quality system documentation, for example to comply with ISO 9000 standards or QS-9000 requirements. For both, a series of intranet pages or menus can be designed to link higher tier documents to lower tier ones. For example, clicking on a link embedded with the purchasing section in a quality system manual brings up a standard operating procedure on purchase orders and also work instructions for a buyer position. A world-class, on-line system also includes links to related forms and data, such as vendor qualification forms and records of contract reviews. Both related current and archived records are readily accessible. A powerful search engine is integrated into the system. The benefits of such a system are accessible, current document versions; no manuals for users to maintain; printing on demand; reduced costs; reduced time from document approval to publication; and faster and less frustrating searching.

C. System Features

Before organizations invest in hardware and software to convert their hard copy documentation, they would be wise to compare a list of world-class system features with their customers' requirements and their own current ability to meet those needs. Organizations considering establishing an on-line system should modify the list based on their customers' requirements and documentation function. Note that many of the listed features also apply well to CD distribution, an aid to organizations with security-restricted or otherwise limited telecommunications. In this alternative implementation, updated CDs are delivered regularly to replace obsolete ones, which are collected and reused. The following list includes features recommended for information input, access, viewing, searching, printing, storing, logistics, and systems support.

Input

Input features for a standardized storage and retrieval system focus on protecting information from unauthorized revision, two-way communication with customers, timely review, and specialized training.

"Locking" information through software and restricting input access to a few individuals, but including at least one backup, is essential to maintaining document integrity. Documents on the system are read-only to everyone else. The system should also allow distributed input, which means authorized personnel at multiple locations can add, revise, or delete information. For example, a revision to the quality system manual may come from the quality assurance department or documentation function, or a job description may be uploaded in HR. In a distributed input system, entering information for each document is restricted specifically to that document.

Another input feature is the capacity for interaction, for example, to allow viewers to transmit questions and comments and to allow providers to respond. Often, response boxes are integrated into the system. This feature is used frequently to request items, such as preprinted forms or charts, that may be unavailable on-line.

**Checklist 4.2:
Characteristics of a
Document Storage
and Retrieval System**

Input

- ☐ Protected, read-only
- ☐ Distributed
- ☐ Capacity for interaction, such as query and response forms
- ☐ Compatible with "tickler" software
- ☐ Specialized training

Access

- ☐ Link or jump readily between other applications
- ☐ Link or jump readily between other documents
- ☐ No special user password required
- ☐ Usage can be monitored
- ☐ Multiple computing platforms, if needed
- ☐ Compatible with company standard software
- ☐ Usable from/to remote sites
- ☐ Handles simultaneous users without queuing or slowing
- ☐ Reliable communications networks
- ☐ LAN accessible

☐ Internet or intranet

☐ Terminals in common areas

Viewing

☐ Graphical user interface (GUI)

☐ Graphics compatible with users' hardware and software

☐ WYSIWYG (what you see [on the screen] is what you get)

☐ Text emphasis, such as underline, bold, italics

☐ Special characters, such as dashes, slashes

☐ Document number, date, and screen or page number

☐ Passive notification of revisions

☐ Addition, revision screens, and cancellation screens

☐ Automatic update of addition, revision, and cancellation screens

Searching

☐ Context specific

☐ Language relationships

Printing

☐ To e-mail

☐ By document

☐ By screen

Compatibility with "tickler" software is an important input feature where providers are responsible for notifying personnel of document review dates at regular intervals. For example, if operating procedures specify that a document needs to be reviewed at least once every two years, the system should be able to integrate information accessed in advance with tickler software so staff will not have to reenter the same document information, such as document title, number, and review due date.

Systems that include or have options for training translate into smoother and quicker conversions from hard copy to on-line. Training for those responsible for inputting documents pays off.

Access

Several considerations for choosing a standardized, on-line system involve viewer access. The common denominator of the features is people-friendly access, which means compatibility, comfort, speed, and reliability. These features emphasize easy and fast movement between related applications and from document to document.

The best on-line systems allow users to link or jump readily between applications and documents, for example, from a standard operating procedure produced in a word processing program to a signature authority chart created in spreadsheet software. An intranet link can be constructed between the part of a procedure that specifies a form and the part of a signature authority chart that lists the approval required for that specific form. Another example of this feature applies to a hierarchy of quality system documentation compliant with ISO 9000 standards: links between the quality system manual, standard operating procedures, and work instructions. Some of the most challenging links or jumps, however, are between unrelated systems, such as material handling or accounting systems and standard operating procedures.

To encourage users to access documents, and to avoid costly maintenance, avoid issuing special passwords for viewing. Either have a common password for all users (especially on a system where limited access is desired for some information), or configure a system to require no password.

To obtain data for continuous improvement to documentation, for example, to learn which documents are accessed and how often, include a feature that tallies usage by document group and specific document, such as all standard operating procedures or just procedure X.

Although desktop computers are moving toward operating seamlessly between platforms, such as PC and Macintosh, standardized hardware reduces time and cost of processes associated with access, for example, delivering training and preparing published instructions. Legacy systems, especially where a significant number and location of mainframe terminals are users' only access, amplify the need for a document storage and retrieval system that is compatible with multiple platforms.

Another feature of a world-class documentation system is standard software, whose benefits extend beyond the storage and retrieval system. Merged and reengineered organizations, understandably, sometimes are reluctant to adopt standard, organizationwide software, because of the inconvenience and initial investment of resources needed for conversion.

Successful storage and retrieval systems address an organization's need for remote site access. As organizations expand globally, remote access becomes an increasingly frequent need. Where secure information is not required, Internet access is an option. For restricted access, LANs and intranets may be alternatives, where permitted. Some organizations access documentation through modems with a system that has protected call-back features. CDs distributed by conventional channels can substitute for on-line access, but their use involves considerable regular maintenance. The fewest different means for access generally provide the greatest time and cost efficiency.

On-line systems should be able to handle multiple users simultaneously without queuing or slowing access. Organizations are wise to investigate the

- ☐ Hard copy on demand (discouraged wholesale printing)
- ☐ Document number, date, and page

Storing

- ☐ Cost
- ☐ Transmission ease
- ☐ Protection
- ☐ Audit trails
- ☐ Retrieval ease

Logistics

- ☐ Ease of use
- ☐ Cost:
    - ☐ Conversion
    - ☐ System purchase
    - ☐ Upgrades
- ☐ Alternatives for closed areas
- ☐ Electronic coordination and approval

limits of their existing and proposed telecommunications resources, hardware, and documentation software. Document storage and retrieval systems that work well for organizations with several hundred employees sometimes fail with several thousand. Similarly configured organizations often can provide the most helpful data toward selecting the best system.

Easy, fast, and dependable on-line access can be no better than the weakest link in an organization's communications network. Functions that require close to 100 percent up time, such as visitor authorization in a secure facility, will want to consider the reliability of communications in planning a system or deciding whether to retain backup hard copy at users' locations—in this instance, at plant entrances.

A final consideration of access relates to common viewing stations. Although office workers generally have access to a personal or easily shared computer terminal, specialized manufacturing facilities, outdoor locations, and other work sites may prohibit close-at-hand electronic access. One solution is to install terminals in protected common areas where employees can access on-line documents. Cafeterias and break rooms, libraries, field office trailers, and central corridors are a few locations where employees can have common access.

Viewing

System features that allow all users to view information as intended are the most satisfactory and the most economical to maintain. Whenever special processes need to be implemented for just some users, the resulting variability introduces opportunities for errors and requires additional maintenance activity. For instance, two different sets of instructions may have to be written and maintained for viewing intranet documents at workstations that can display sophisticated graphics and those that cannot. The next best situation to standardized viewing capabilities is accommodating those differences, for example, embedding alternative directions where the graphics were intended to be seen. Unacceptable systems permit some stations to display a document as intended, and others to fill a screen with gibberish instead. People-friendliness is the common denominator of features for viewing documents, described next, just as it is with access.

GUI or point-and-click technology is more or less taken for granted these days. Some systems, however, require commands for viewing on-line documents. Users accustomed to GUI viewing generally dislike command systems, to put it mildly. Especially if the system is used infrequently, which is often the case with corporate directive documents, commands are cumbersome. Some systems compromise by presenting viewing commands on every screen. A less satisfactory compromise is presenting on every screen a command that can be used to jump to a menu that defines all viewing commands.

Seldom do entire organizations purchase or upgrade their computers at the same time, except for small organizations and startups. Therefore, on-line documents usually are viewed through a variety of hardware and sometimes software. Graphics, such as logos and diagrams, that are legible on one monitor may be fuzzy, slow to appear, or not viewable at all on another. System standardization may require adding memory, upgrading video cards, or other modifications to handle graphics satisfactorily. Where upgrades are not feasible, care should be taken when inputting documents to ensure that the least sophisticated equipment can display all graphics. That may mean simplifying some documents or document formats.

WYSIWYG (pronounced *whizzy wig*) stands for What You See Is What You Get. It means that a printed document looks exactly like it appears on a screen. Some systems do not deliver WYSIWYG to all workstations. Although not as common as a few years ago, screen-to-printout mismatches are still frustrating and can lead to withdrawal of support for on-line document systems. Documents sent through e-mail systems occasionally also have WYSIWYG difficulties.

A system should be able to display emphasized text, for example, bold, underline, and italics. PDF documents, described earlier, are one solution, but workstations need to have software with PDF reading capabilities.

Special characters, such as dashes and slashes, may interfere with some system programming, but usually are not a problem with popular desktop applications.

Document numbers and revision dates on every page or screen, and page or screen numbers of total pages or screens (such as page 2 of 4), help viewers manage documentation. If a person needs to leave a screen temporarily, for instance to answer a telephone call, he or she can resume viewing activity quickly without needing to press keys to find out where he or she is.

Another helpful feature is to notify viewers passively when a document is revised, a new document is added, or an existing document is deleted. Passive notification means the user doesn't have to query the system to learn of changes. E-mail notification is one vehicle for this feature. E-mailed distribution can be customized according to document subject. For example, notice of revisions to documents in one manual, such as calibration procedures, can be sent only to employees involved in calibration processes. This feature is especially useful for reviewing a document prior to on-line publication; only key personnel receive notification of the changes to be reviewed. Alternatively, the entire document may be sent electronically to selected reviewers.

Inclusion of addition, revision, and cancellation screens aids viewers who may be unable to access the system for a considerable period of time, such as during vacations, leaves, or travel. Intranets can have links to such screens and also can link directly to the referenced documents or to explanations for their cancellation. Rolling 12-week windows have worked well for many organizations. These screens and links usually are updated weekly, but can be updated according to the volume and frequency of changes. To reduce maintenance activity, screens and links can be programmed to update automatically as documents are revised on the system.

Searching

A few years ago, information providers had to enter key words for each document into the system one by one, and retrieval was limited to individual words or phrases. Software now has powerful search engines that are sensitive to context and language relationships. For example, by typing in the word *retail* and excluding *Retail Division,* a user can display all documents that address a company's retail issues, but not the many documents that include Retail Division, such as in the document headers of a Retail Division procedures manual. Viewers no longer have to guess the exact words the technical writer used in a document; instead, the system can display documents containing synonyms or other related terms. Software can locate information hierarchically related to entered words. For instance, if *banana* is entered, it can display information about *fruit* (more general) or about *plantains* (more specific), a type of banana. Programs can even show the various weighting of different documents—in other words, can arrange them by likely relevance. The best systems not only display documents, but zero in on places in the documents, paragraphs, and sentences where the searched information can be found.

Many Internet and intranet browsers offer excellent search capabilities. Some can be used to search an entire document system; others are organized by topic or by document subgroups (see Resources).

At the most basic level, documents can be searched using common word processing software; however, organizing them as master documents with subdocuments allows greater search capabilities, for example, sections within a manual. The biggest disadvantage to searching with word processing software alone is being unable to search across an entire manual or document system.

Printing

Printing on demand and to a variety of media is an important system feature and is readily available through specialized storage and retrieval software. However, the capability to print out a whole manual with a mouse click or single command may be counterproductive. Consideration should be given to configuring the system to restrict wholesale printing, especially when an organization is converting from a hard copy system to on-line. Making it easy to subvert electronic document storage and retrieval presents neither the access, cost, or other benefits of on-line, nor the advantages of a well-organized hard copy manual.

Capabilities should include printing by document, page, and screen, and printing to e-mail (send documents as attachments). The system should also automatically print the document number, date, and page on each page printed out. Without that information, obsolete individual pages may find their way into reports and correspondence and compromise document integrity.

Storing

Document storage and retrieval systems should meet several requirements, including cost, transmission ease, protection, audit trails, and retrieval ease.

Efficient systems transmit documents electronically from desktop to storage, usually by a LAN or other network, thereby minimizing handling costs, such as with disks. Although early mainframe systems required information providers to learn complex uploading and editing commands, contemporary systems feature easy point-and-click file transfers to a storage server. On-site servers and mainframe computers can be short-term repositories, and hardware at remote sites can meet long-term storage needs. Often—especially for smaller organizations—the server is little more than a high-capacity desktop computer, thereby containing system costs.

Sound storage and retrieval systems require the preservation of document integrity, including restricted ability to add, revise, or delete documents. They also provide protection in the event of a disaster, such as fire and flooding. Saving files to floppy disks kept near a hard drive may be convenient, and unfortunately is one of the most common kinds of storage systems, but it is risky. The frequency of backing up documents depends on the volume and frequency of revisions. Regularly scheduled daily or weekly backups work well for large organizations with fairly dynamic documentation systems. Smaller organizations undergoing major reorganization or process improvements also benefit from frequent backups. The more automated the procedure, the greater the likelihood of consistent backups (see Chapter 8 for more information on storage).

Maintaining document audit trails is another critical feature of a storage and retrieval system. Earlier revisions and both merged and deleted documents can be archived automatically by the system and retrievable within a reasonable time frame. To meet the requirements of ISO 9000, and good business practice, archived documents should be marked clearly to avoid confusing them with current documents, and history files should be traceable forward and backward.

Retrieval from electronic document storage can eliminate the requirement for multiple filing and can introduce other efficiencies. For example, large organizations often issue organization charts by department. To facilitate retrieval, because of investigations or other litigation activity, they are often duplicated and filed both by department and date. Typical investigations need to determine the reporting structure in place at a given time, but some need to trace a particular department's reorganizations. Electronic storage and retrieval requires only single entries, or uploading, of the charts and permits sorting and retrieval either by date or department or some other attribute. Electronic retrieval should be fast and reliable.

Logistics

Practical considerations for an electronic document storage and retrieval system include ease of use (minimal training required); reasonable costs for conversion, system purchase, and upgrade; electronic coordination and approval; and alternatives for secure areas.

A system with the most sophisticated search capabilities and most features may be frustrating and costly if users require prolonged training. Such a system often also drains MIS help desk resources. Organizations should also consider the expense of converting their existing document systems; the cost of purchasing hardware, software, and licensing agreements; and the often overlooked anticipated expense of upgrades. Questions to ask include: How often are upgrades issued, and how extensive and expensive have they been in the past?

Another practical consideration is document coordination and approval. Typically, company documents require review and approval of several functions. A policy on employee training, for example, may be reviewed by HR, quality assurance, contracts, and purchasing functions. The hard copy approval process could be both paper- and time-consuming. Revisions are duplicated and mailed with a cover/response page. Reviewers comment or mark up the hard copy, usually duplicate and file their input, and mail the revision. Document coordination personnel compile responses and then reconcile differences among reviewers by telephone or meeting or they mail a new revision.

With electronic coordination and approval, document revisions are placed on-line and reviewers are notified through the storage and retrieval system, e-mail, or other electronic means. Reviewers can comment directly on the system, and can view and respond to other reviewers' responses. Software now even allows reviewers to post pseudo yellow self-stick notes directly on the on-line documents. The more sophisticated systems permit electronic approval of the final document, which is then published on the system.

Finally, organizations that have limited or no access to conventional electronic distribution, such as LANs, should consider the practicality of alternative distribution, such as CDs. Systems that allow easy information transfer to alternative document delivery are worth seeking for such organizations.

Systems Support

Organizations that have an internal information systems function often can provide the technical support to install, customize, and manage an on-line document storage and retrieval system. Frequently, however, internal MIS functions are challenged to meet existing demands and are unavailable to take on the project. Two alternatives to internal support include outsourcing the application or hiring consultants temporarily to establish the system, who then turn it over to internal personnel to manage. The second track of

The Aerospace Corporation's policies and practices improvement effort, establishing an on-line system, was supported by the corporation's computer information resources department. The policies and practices team chartered a subteam to develop and implement the system. Members of the subteam included the computer information resources personnel, representatives from the corporate directives function, and other members of the policies and practices team, including the project consultant. The following list of major activities the subteam requested of information resources personnel could be a blueprint for other organizations seeking the same kind of support.

- Assign an information resources department project manager to coordinate computer services support for accessing and searching corporate policies and practices on the organization's intranet.

- Consult with the policies and practices improvement team leader to schedule activities that result in on-line, searchable access to the streamlined policies and practices by a given date.

- Install server software and all software needed by at least one representative in each department for browsing, searching, displaying, and printing corporate policies and practices.

- Advise the team on access alternatives for closed areas, for example, disks or CDs.

- Establish and document uploading procedures for corporate directives staff, including new or revised documents and cancellations.

- Advise the team on procedures and provide necessary support for e-mail notification of new or revised policies and practices and cancellations.

- Advise corporate directives staff on e-mail transfer of files to individual requesters.

- Establish and maintain hotline support during the installation of the on-line system. Maintain data and provide reports of problems and questions to be used to continuously improve the system and indicate training requirements.

- Train users in accessing and searching documents. Train corporate directives staff in uploading documents.

- Maintain data on document hits.

- Establish procedures for electronic archiving, and recommend off-site storage for disaster recovery.

D. The Case for Imaging

As long-term storage of hard copy records becomes more and more costly, businesses are turning to electronic imaging to capture, retain, and retrieve information. In the most basic terms, digital images of documents are comprised of tiny picture elements (pixels), which can be manipulated electronically. Imaging systems can reduce the cost of handling hard copy documents by saving filing time and space, and retrieval time. Images commonly are captured from hard copy by scanning, although other capture devices, such as video, fax, and X-ray also are used.

Is electronic imaging too good to be true? The answer is both "no" and "yes." It can be a reasonable alternative to hard copy document processing, especially if an organization's storage costs are high in relation to its labor costs (converting hard copies to electronic images can be labor-intensive), if document access speed is critical to business goals, and if knowledgeable personnel are available to ensure that storage media remain compatible with retrieval hardware and software and are stable over time. Imaging hardware and software vendors sometimes promote their products and services without communicating clearly all the costs of implementing a system; frequently, organizations are surprised by the staff power required to scan existing documents into the system. Where organizations can store essential records inexpensively (for example, using off-site warehouses or outsourced facilities) and users can live with retrieval time in hours not minutes, hard copy storage may make more sense economically. And sorry stories abound where organizations stored imaged documents on tapes and disks and other devices for which retrieval hardware was no longer available, or deteriorated, or where the software needed to retrieve imaged documents was no longer available. For imaging to work, someone in the organization needs to be responsible for monitoring the equipment, software, and storage media and advising when conversions to other products would be prudent.

> **Checklist 4.3: Considerations for Electronic Document Imaging**
>
> ☐ Storage costs are high in relation to labor costs.
>
> ☐ Fast access to documents is critical.
>
> ☐ Knowledgeable personnel are available to monitor equipment, software, and media availability and condition.

CHAPTER 5

Measured Improvement

Solutions presented in this chapter address documentation challenges such as

- How to measure the satisfaction of documentation customers
- How to achieve zero defects
- What to do when documentation is too old
- How to reduce processing time
- How to reduce volume
- How to compare the true costs of hard copy and on-line systems

Every major improvement effort, when initiated, strains resources. Like any successful investment, returns come later. Although some process improvements pay off immediately, more take at least a few weeks, and sometimes months, to show results. Functions baseline current processes, and that diverts personnel away from routine assignments. Teams meet to identify causes and trends and generate solutions. Whether preparing for ISO 9000 registration, adding pizzazz to a user's guide to attract consumers, or redesigning a forms management system, change consumes resources, especially when documentation functions have been entrenched in an organization for years and reach far into other functions, such as quality assurance, media, or purchasing. How can an organization justify embarking on a major documentation improvement effort?

The answer is in the nature of today's marketplace, whether global or intradivision or anything in between. The pressure is constant to improve processes. Customers expect higher quality and lower costs. That is as true for a documentation contractor as it is for a company that processes pickles. And measurement is nothing more than a tool to both judge and adjust a course for improvement.

A formula was created to help management (engineering) see the temporary effect of improvement investing. It illustrates increased workload—which translates to expense—of organizations going through change, even though the change will result in reduced workload and expense.

$$W(X, T) = \overline{W}(X) + W'(X, T)$$

W = Workload

X = Organization

T = Time

The workload of a given organization at any time (W) is equal to a steady state workload under quiescent conditions ($\overline{W}$) plus a variable workload attributable to turbulent conditions (change) (W').

Acknowledging the initial but temporary investment in increased workload and expense, this chapter describes processes contributing to improved documentation nimbleness and presents metrics to monitor progress—from baseline data to world-class achievement in customer satisfaction, defect-free documents, and currentness. Then, processes, metrics, and improvements are presented for cycle time, volume, and cost.

A. Customer Satisfaction

In Chapter 2, customers—including external customers, users, and subject matter owners—were among the five sources of need described for documentation. How do we measure customer satisfaction? How do we express improvement?

One way is to give feedback sheets to customers each time a product or service is delivered, and then compile the responses and examine the data for common threads. The neighborhood soup and salad restaurant presents a postage paid card with a dinner check. The furnace repair person leaves the same kind of card. Each time a documentation consulting firm completes a project, it sends a feedback sheet with the invoice. The automobile dealer's service manager calls. An S&P team sends a simple check-off form when it works with subject matter owners to produce or revise their procedures and other documents (see Chapter 2). The team tracked feedback quarterly and found several opportunities to improve service.

When the Hughes Ground Systems Group S&P employees were building senior management commitment for their on-line information storage and retrieval system, they sent a memo to every major function and division head. They asked for feedback. These internal customers, they found, wanted a longer lead time before hard copy manuals were eliminated. However, the S&P team also gained support for the project.

The Videotex support people at Hughes programmed the on-line system to measure document hits, that is, the number of times each screen was viewed. They reported the information monthly to the S&P function, where the data helped shape decisions about documents needed on the system.

Improvement-conscious software manufacturers install help line databases that reveal trends in customers' trouble calls. With enough callers for a problem spot, the company can either improve its software or revise its on-line help function or user manual.

B. Zero Defects

In terms of rework cost and loss of customer satisfaction and image, documentation defects are no different than for any other product or service. Many people believe it is impossible to achieve zero defects. Like any product or service, establishing clear goals according to customers' needs comes first. Then metrics are established, strategies planned and implemented, and results achieved. Defects in documentation include typos; but they also include content inaccuracy, misfiled records, and lost forms. Every defect costs money, but also time to respond to messages about the defect, lost confidence translated into lack of support, and expenses for consumables such as paper and other supplies.

This section focuses on proofreading processes and metrics that helped a documentation function achieve zero defects, primarily in text quality and content accuracy.

Proofreading

To some, three proofreaders for every document seems like overkill. To an organization that knows the cost of rework, confusion, distraction, and even mild annoyance caused by defective documentation, three seems just right.

The following is a funny but true story about a company bulletin about quality. The company's quality division called to alert a documentation function that a bulletin had to be published by 4:00 P.M. the same day. The caller insisted on walking the draft over to the function, which was about a quarter mile away. Huffing and puffing, the anxious caller came with bulletin in hand. "I'd like to look it over, first," the manager told him. "No," he said. "Our division manager already looked it over and signed it, and we don't have time. We have to get this printed and distributed by the afternoon mail run."

With a quick glance at the copy, the manager spotted two errors immediately. Reading that page and the second one carefully produced three more. By now the caller was visibly impatient.

The manager asked, "There was no time to proofread this bulletin, but there is time to fix the mistakes and run back to get a new signature?" By the way, the title of the bulletin was "Total Quality."

Before adopting Nimble Documentation® processes, all Hughes Ground Systems Group S&P analysts gave their work to analyst Bill to proofread. Bill was an excellent proofreader; but nobody else was. So Bill spent a good part of his workday proofreading coworkers' documents. And the people who word processed the drafts always assumed Bill would catch their errors. The arrangement was a perfect example of the traditional inspector-at-the-end-of-the-production-line model.

The function had largely maintained existing processes for more than 25 years and balked at changing the way it worked. Gradually, as the organization attracted attention for its growing practice of continuous measurable improvement, pride overtook resistance. Key to the transformation, which later landed the function a zero-defects award, was a proofreading system that held all participants who added value to a document responsible for the document's quality, starting with the word processing person. In many offices, the person who does word processing is expected to submit a draft to be proofread by someone else. Here, every person was responsible for the quality of his or her own work, and everyone functioned as a receiving inspector. Staff corrected defects early and received feedback early to help detect, correct, and prevent recurring defects. Soon, Bill no longer was the only skilled proofreader. Everyone was.

This is a good place to address the sometimes controversial issue of having text processing personnel prepare documentation. Hardly an office exists where an analyst, engineer, manager, or other document generator isn't preparing a document for publication. Except for very brief or informal documents, it is wise and cost-effective to have specially trained text processing professionals rather than other staff do the final formatting. For one, text processing specialists are skilled in the sophisticated features of word processing software that can save time and reduce errors. Two, who is generating the drafts, designing, or supervising while analysts, engineers, and supervisors spend hours adjusting margins or working with other document formatting features? And last, can competitive organizations continue to afford compensating highly paid personnel for work that is better accomplished by others? It is satisfying to produce a finished document. It introduces closure to sometimes abstract, vague, and elusive assignments. However, unless the therapeutic effect upon document generators to final format a document is more important than time, quality, and cost efficiencies, documentation functions should seriously consider including assigning work to text processing specialists.

Although requiring more than one proofreader for each procedure may seem unnecessary and wasteful, eliminated rework proved its worth. (The quality community reminds us that an error corrected during processing costs 10 times the price of an error prevented. And the cost once the product is delivered—document published—is 100 times!)

The system included a document cover sheet (synopsis sheet) that identified the staff responsible for proofreading: word processing person (proofreader 1), analyst (proofreader 2), and second analyst (proofreader 3). A major part of the system was a checklist for countable errors (developed by the function) and monthly metrics charting the function's progress. The checklist, an application of a widely known quality control tool, was designed after pilot data showed defect trends. For example, errors were more likely in text outside the body of a practice or bulletin, such as a document number or title. Proofreaders tallied any errors they found. Each used a different color pen and gave feedback to the others. The proofreading improvement effort also included training sessions with a corporate communications editor, and, later, desk instructions.

In less than a year, average monthly defect rates dropped from more than two per page to fewer than one per 20 pages, and those defects tended to be extremely minor, such as a single incidence of three rather than two spaces between sentences. As defects approached zero, the system was modified to sampling pages at increasing intervals, with no significant increase in errors. Because of the feedback and training, error-free work became the organizational standard, staff members became more skilled in producing error-free work the first time, and cycle time decreased for processing documents.

You may be asking, "What about spellcheck?" or "So what is the big deal over a few typos?" Word processing software's spellcheck feature was part of the proofreading process, but was inadequate. Some features today address some of the checklist entries, such as duplicate words (*the the*), but many errors still pass through spellcheck filters. For example, popular word processing software does not flag punctuation or format inconsistencies or word transpositions. Grammar checkers do identify some problems, such as noun-verb agreement, but also suggest that so many correct constructions are incorrect that documentation specialists usually find it easier not to use them.

In the Hughes example, because most documents were distributed to more than 1000 employees, any error resulted in at least half a dozen telephone calls, which took staff time to respond to. Errors also tarnished the image of the function, which was more than merely a cosmetic concern. That's not to say a typo had the same effect as a display advertisement seen recently in a regional newspaper. That department store ad featured a sale on hosiery, unfortunately listed as *Pestilence,* when what it probably meant was *Resilience*! However, even when the typo potential is not as sorrowful, a reputation for professionalism and skill goes a long way to obtaining support and commitment for resources to maintain and improve service. Customer trust is at stake, which is especially important as internal documentation functions compete for shrinking resources and with outside suppliers. Even a minor typographical error, if repeated, plants a question in customers' minds: If they're sloppy about typos, are they sloppy about content, too? Workmanship pride also can contribute to sustained quality.

Every documentation organization that adopts a similar system will have different countables, depending upon the nature of the documents, skills of the staff, and improvement goals. Figure 5.1 shows the tally sheet that worked for this organization.

The same function developed proofreading desk instructions to document its processes and help train new staff. Figure 5.2 is a copy of the S&P organization's proofreading desk instructions. Figure 5.3 shows proofreading desk instructions after a mainframe on-line system was implemented and the organization saw the need to control errors that slipped in before and during uploading processes. Both systems were adopted before development

Month _____

First proofreader												
Second proofreader												
Third proofreader												
CONTENT												**TOTAL**
Missing information												
Inaccurate information												
Clarity (phrase or sentence)												
Unclear referent												
Poorly organized paragraph												
Wrong word												
Other content defect												
SPELLING												
Title misspelling												
Heading misspelling												
Body misspelling												
Name misspelling												
Footnote misspelling												
Other misspelling												
MECHANICS												
Doubling												
Roman/Arabic numerals												
Inconsistent hyphenation												
Noun-verb disagreement												
And/or												
Capitalization												
Pagination												
Inconsistent use of colon												
Inconsistent use of period												
Inconsistent headings												
Inconsistent underline												
Transposition												
Unnecessary *Denotes revision*												
Other mechanics defects												
FORMAT												
Uneven margins												
Brackets												
Misaligned paragraph number or letter												
Letter spacing												
Line spacing												
Form of date												
Other format defects												
PAGE TALLY												

Figure 5.1. S&P proofreading defect classifications.

1. The analyst receives a hard copy or disk, or both, of the new or revised document draft. (Note: The analyst may be helping to originate or revise a document. Also, where a document already exists on the S&P system, the analyst copies the document to his or her desktop to make changes to it.)

2. Where there are minor changes, the analyst edits the document and may make those changes, which are then submitted to the text processor electronically to format and finalize on the S&P system.

   Where there are major changes or complete typing of new documents, the analyst edits and submits the redlined hard copy or disk, or both, to the text processor for typing and formatting on the S&P system.

3. The analyst notifies the text processor that the document is ready for finalization.

4. The text processor copies the document submitted by the analyst to the S&P system.

5. The text processor proofs the document, prints a hard copy of the document, and submits it to the analyst for proofing.

6. The analyst proofs the document and forwards it to the second analyst to proofread.

7. The analyst submits the document to the originator or executive for signature approval.

Figure 5.2. S&P proofreading instructions.

The following instructions provide guidance to the S&P Department for proofreading practices, procedures, bulletins, and statements of responsibility (SORs) before release, to ensure accuracy and clarity.

Text Processors

1. After completing text processing and before printing out a hard copy for proofing, run spellcheck. Proofread the document. If only minor corrections are detected during proofreading, make them on the draft copy but do not make corrections on the Microsoft Word disk until the analyst has also proofread the document (this reduces the number of correction cycles).

2. When the analyst indicates a copy is needed for approval signature, incorporate the final changes, run a final Spellcheck, proofread and mark corrections, and return the package to the analyst for proofing. After the analyst has proofed the document, incorporate the accumulated changes.

Figure 5.3. S&P proofreading instructions (for mainframe on-line publication).

Analysts

1. Proofread all drafts, using S&P standard editing marks, and return the drafts to the text processor to incorporate changes.

2. To obtain a final copy of the document for approval, perform the following.

    a. Have a second analyst proofread the document (using a different color pen).

    b. If changes are minor, submit the document (with completed Synopsis Sheet) to final proofreader for review and approval.

    c. Note: If the document is an Attachment or Maintenance Revision, a Synopsis Sheet is not required. The final proofreader indicates approval on the Data Processing and Review Record (DPRR).

    d. If changes are extensive, have the text processor incorporate changes before submittal to final proofreader. (Use discretion on obtaining a second-analyst proofing again.)

    e. After the final proofreader's review, submit the document to the text processor for incorporation of final changes.

    f. After the final proofreader's approval and incorporation of final changes, submit the document and Synopsis Sheet to the designated executive for approval.

3. When the hard copy is received from the information provider with confirmation on the DPRR that it has been uploaded in Videotex, proofread the following items.

    a. The document, comparing it with the hard copy to be sure all the information is accurate. Also confirm key word accuracy, using a copy of the key word list supplied by the information provider and comparing it with the key words written on the DPRR.

    b. Changes to the Table of Contents.

    c. Changes to the 12-week screen.

S&P Manager

Reviews documents received from analysts and indicates approval by signing and dating the Synopsis Sheet (DPRR for Attachments and Maintenance Revisions).

Information Providers

After the document is uploaded into Videotex, proofread the document, comparing it to the hard copy for accuracy and confirming that all screen information is correct. Also, confirm that key words are accurate by comparing them with the key words written on the DPRR.

Information providers should also proofread changes to the Table of Contents and changes to the 12-week screen.

Figure 5.3. *Continued.*

of the sophisticated software and LANs that feature on-line group editing and revision. The function, now consolidated with several others, is studying conversion to a client-server environment and intranet-based or other updated document access system.

C. Currentness

Blink, and technology zooms by. Yet company systems and procedures often grow mold. Worse, cumbersome and obsolete documentation snubs customers and suffocates employees—and may be a resource bomb waiting to be detonated by the next legal challenge.

Maintaining current documentation balances between the need for up-to-the-minute documents and available resources. When laws change, documents such as a city's no-smoking policy may need to change immediately. And establishing an annual review cycle for all policies, practices, and procedures helps prevent document obsolescence. A document that is worth keeping is worth keeping up to date. But if an organization is fairly stable, and processes do not change much, adopting a review cycle of 24 months and perhaps even 36 months may be adequate.

Design metrics to baseline the currentness of policies, practices, procedures, and other directive documents. Then regularly collect data and chart the organization's progress toward eliminating the oldest documents, assuming critical ones are reviewed first. Naturally, after a major documentation improvement effort, all of the documents will be current. Establish objectives to continue to monitor currentness and raise red flags when documents begin to age. In many organizations, documentation is a low priority, at least until audits or legal claims strike; so use currentness metrics to nudge subject matter experts to review documents to keep them up to date. Figure 5.4 shows metrics for currentness of policies and practices at the start of a major improvement project.

D. Cycle Time

Documents that take a long time to write, edit, coordinate, and publish frustrate writers and users. Keeping track of processing cycle time may reveal some surprises and may spur staff into searching for non–value-added processes and ways to improve the documentation management system. If nothing else, the metrics bring attention to functions that tend to delay the review process and motivate them to place a higher priority on reviewing drafts.

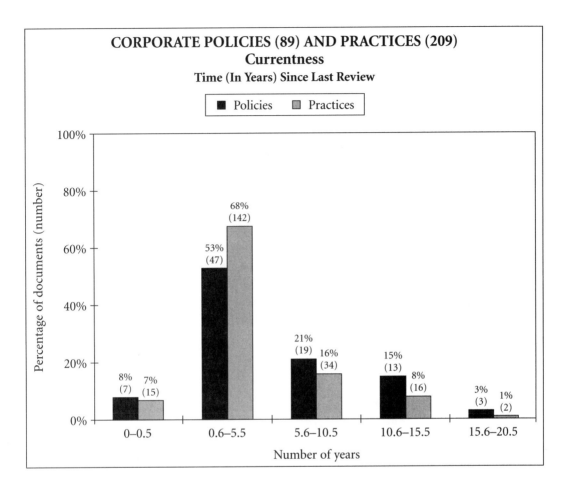

Figure 5.4. Metrics for currentness.

A Hughes team benchmarked coordination time for policies and practices with several companies in Southern California, mostly in the defense electronics industry, and researched industry data. Although the industry figures might have improved recently along with more companies' adoption of quality management, the comparison in 1995 is worth looking at. Documents took a whopping average of six months to coordinate. In the cycle time chart, an Aerospace Corporation team superimposed the industry data on its achievement in reducing coordination time for corporate policies and practices (see Figure 5.5). What harm can come from a six-month average? Laws and regulations change. Companies reorganize. Customers' requirements change. Competition increases. It behooves a documentation function to process and publish directive documentation quickly.

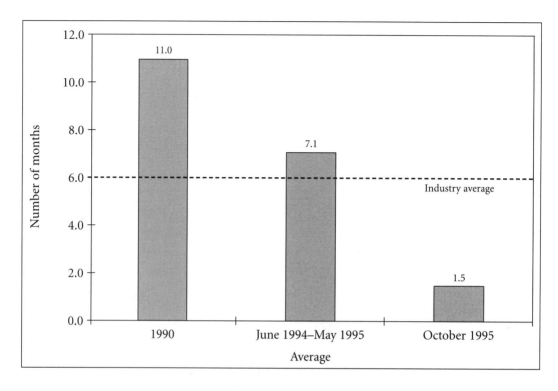

Figure 5.5. Corporate policies and practices: Coordination and approval.

Another team at a different company tracked document backlog during a major documentation conversion to an on-line system. These metrics helped the team members plan their work and respond to customers. The actual data are unavailable; however, metrics for sample data are presented in Figure 5.6.

Subject matter experts told a support team they needed practices and bulletins uploaded more quickly to the on-line document storage and retrieval system. The support team baselined the cycle time for uploading documents and charted its metrics. By identifying value-added and non–value-added activities, and obtaining additional technical training, the team members succeeded in reducing the average uploading time from about 2.5 *days* to about 30 *minutes* (see Figure 5.7). The customers were pleased.

E. Volume

Directive documentation, whether hard copy or on-line, is expensive to maintain. More documents are more expensive to maintain. More also

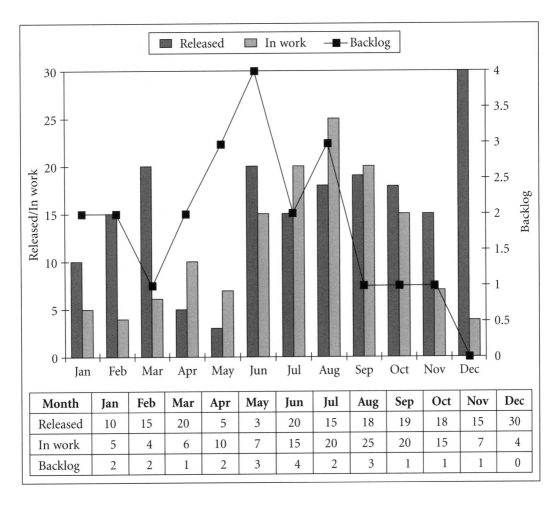

Month	Jan	Feb	Mar	Apr	May	Jun	Jul	Aug	Sep	Oct	Nov	Dec
Released	10	15	20	5	3	20	15	18	19	18	15	30
In work	5	4	6	10	7	15	20	25	20	15	7	4
Backlog	2	2	1	2	3	4	2	3	1	1	1	0

Figure 5.6. Sample data: Items released, in work, and backlog.

increase liability. The potential for successful grievances and lawsuits goes up as volume increases. However, even if litigation is unsuccessful, businesses pay dearly. The compensation clock keeps ticking while staff research and prepare defenses. And documents that employees fail to follow are mine fields waiting for footsteps. Documents are easy targets for auditors; so, typically, many procedures are written in direct response to audit findings. Over time, the procedures accumulate. Manuals get fat.

Monitoring the number of documents and pages and estimating the costs of processing and maintaining them provide important feedback for improvement. Data provide incentives to control volume and, therefore, maintenance costs and liability. Regularly reported volume metrics also

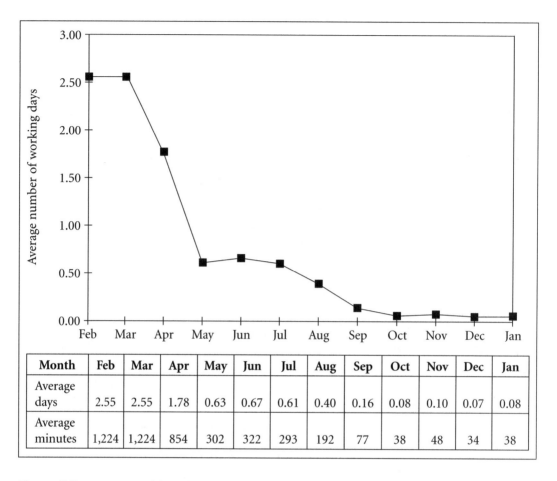

Month	Feb	Mar	Apr	May	Jun	Jul	Aug	Sep	Oct	Nov	Dec	Jan
Average days	2.55	2.55	1.78	0.63	0.67	0.61	0.40	0.16	0.08	0.10	0.07	0.08
Average minutes	1,224	1,224	854	302	322	293	192	77	38	48	34	38

Figure 5.7. Average monthly cycle time for uploading practices and bulletins (from receipt to on-line publication).

motivate teams to continue their zeal in applying the litmus test to all requests for new documents or for expansive revisions to existing ones. Figure 5.8, which shows a simple chart for measuring the continuous reduction of an organization's product operations procedures, is an example of volume metrics.

World-class documentation functions generate volume metrics at the start of their documentation streamlining effort (baseline chart) and at regular intervals thereafter. Baseline metrics that include current volume and targets for reducing volume keep the goal in view of progress. Both Hughes and The Aerospace Corporation generated charts similar to Figure 5.9, which graph baseline, current, and target documentation volume.

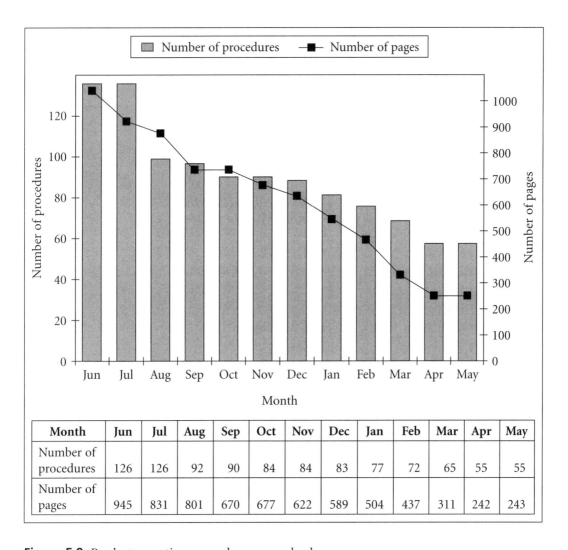

Month	Jun	Jul	Aug	Sep	Oct	Nov	Dec	Jan	Feb	Mar	Apr	May
Number of procedures	126	126	92	90	84	84	83	77	72	65	55	55
Number of pages	945	831	801	670	677	622	589	504	437	311	242	243

Figure 5.8. Product operations procedures manual volume.

F. Cost: The Iceberg Model

Organizations considering an on-line document storage and retrieval system often cite cost as a reason to reject or postpone converting their hard copy system. They name the following costs: hardware, software, telecommunications, technical support, text conversion, training, and other expenses. A counter argument usually includes saving paper and printing costs. It might also include the expense of internal distribution or mailing services to satellite sites. The on-line argument, however, rarely includes the hidden costs.

Think of an iceberg. The really dangerous part is beneath the surface of the water. The part you don't see can do the most damage, whether we are

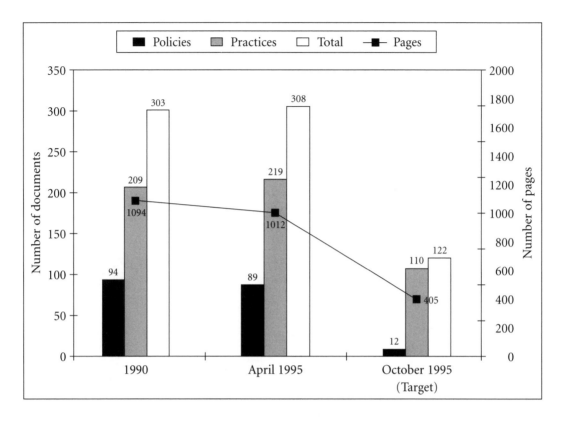

Figure 5.9. Baseline and target volume metrics.

talking about icebergs or documentation system costs (see Figure 5.10). Revisions to hard copy documents are particularly costly. With each revision, someone drafts a change notice or revised document. Then the person text processes the draft notice or revision (or drafts and text processes at the same time). Then someone copies the revision and someone distributes the copies to gain approval of all the functions involved in the change. The processes are repeated after comments arrive regarding the proposed revision. Once the final copies are distributed, someone removes and discards the obsolete copy from each manual and then files the new document. Think of the cost of these hidden processes. But there's more.

Before the draft ever gets to the text processing stage, someone has to research the changes to see if they conflict with or impact other existing information. So they have to search other manuals and documents manually or file by file if the documents are on computer disks. Someone has to update the index. In many organizations, copies of draft revisions awaiting review and final document copies both dive to the bottom of the in-basket stack.

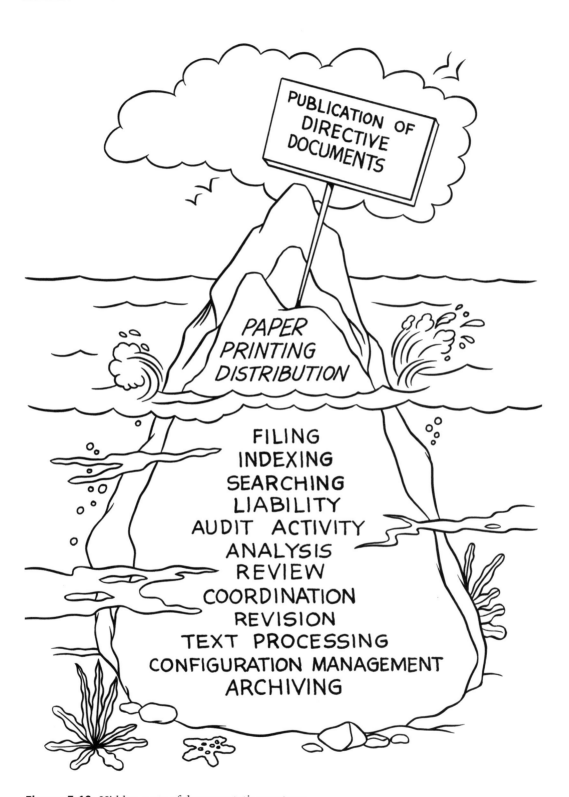

Figure 5.10. Hidden costs of documentation systems.

Reviewing drafts tends to have a low priority. However, maintaining manuals tends to have an even lower priority. Therefore, many manuals wait to be updated, and the result is increased liability and sometimes increased audit activity because of the delays. For all of the hidden factors, the break-even point of converting to an on-line document storage and retrieval system may be closer than most people realize.

Suppose an organization has an on-line documentation system. Is the true (read complete) cost known to add, revise, or even cancel a document? (Yes, cancellations can be costly. See the flowchart example in the Format section (B) of Chapter 3 to trace the processes that may be involved in canceling a document.) Many companies pay for their documentation function with general administration funds and may not source expenses down to the level of the function. Even the organizations that do source expenses to that level seldom measure the cost of processing a document. Knowing little about the cost of processing an average document is a considerable disadvantage for introducing and implementing improvement initiatives. And the ignorance bypasses one of the biggest incentives to streamlining a documentation function: cost. Cost metrics for documentation can support decisions to outsource or insource (see Chapter 9).

Figure 5.11 shows a cost model that can help a company compute the true expense of its corporate policies and practices and that can be adapted to compare the cost of an existing hard copy system against an on-line one. It can be used also to discourage the addition of a document of questionable need. The model divides costs elements by a corporate function that prepares documentation and the company overall. Organizations that have no separate documentation function can combine the model's two parts.

Preparation Function

a. Number of new documents, revisions, and cancellations per [time unit] _____

b. Average time for preparing each new document, revision, and cancellation _____

c. Burdened labor rates for preparation: analysis, writing, text processing, coordination, editing, proofreading, filing, archiving _____

d. Average time for revising index _____

e. Burdened labor rate for revising index _____

Figure 5.11. Cost model for corporate policies and practices.

Company Overall

f. Average time for reviewing and approving each new document, revision, and cancellation   _____

g. Burdened labor rate for approvals   _____

h. Average distribution (number of copies) of new documents, revisions, cancellations, and indices   _____

i. Number of new manuals issued per [time unit]   _____

j. Cost of printing and distributing each new manual   _____

k. Frequency of revision distribution per [time unit]   _____

l. Average cost of printing each new or revised document, cancellation notice, or key word index   _____

m. Average time per new or revised document to file or discard and revise manual index   _____

n. Average burdened labor rate for revision maintainers   _____

o. Average cost of distributing each revision at [headquarters]   _____

p. Average cost of distributing each revision to [other sites]   _____

q. Cost of additional copies (duplication, labor, postage)   _____

r. Average number of searches per [time unit]   _____

s. Average time for each search   _____

t. Average burdened labor rate for searches per [time unit]   _____

Notes:

1. Adjust element assignment to function (Preparation Function versus Company Overall) to reflect existing responsibilities.

2. Depending on the team's requirements for close estimation balanced against the time to collect data, a few additional elements may be factored in such as time and cost of

    • Printing and distributing coordination copies

    • Inquiries and responses

    • Alternatives to policies and practices (because of obsolescence, difficult access)

    • Any electronic text retrieval processing (uploading, copying to disk, tape, and so on)

    • Audit activity

    • Liability

    • Rework

Add floor space cost of manuals if it is a significant cost.

Figure 5.11. *Continued.*

Basic Costs [per time unit]: (Insert other elements as required)

Cost for preparation function:

(__a__ * __b__ * __c__) +

(__a__ * __d__ * __e__) =   _____

Cost for company overall:

(__a__ * __f__ * __g__) +

(__h__ * __k__ * __l__) +

(__i__ * __j__) +

(__h__ * __m__ * __n__) +

(__h_o__ * __o__) +

(__h_p__ * __p__) +

__q__   +

(__r__ * __s__ * __t__) =   _____

Directions

1. Transfer into the formula the amounts for each letter. h_o means with respect to [headquarters]. h_p means with respect to [other sites].

2. The asterisk (*) means multiply. First multiply all numbers within each set of parentheses.

3. Then add the resulting products together.

Figure 5.11. *Continued.*

PART III

Application

CHAPTER 6

Quality Initiatives

Solutions presented in this chapter address documentation challenges such as

- What is the difference between ISO 9001, 9002, and 9003?
- What are the document and records requirements of ISO 9001?
- How does the Baldrige Award compare with ISO 9000 standards?
- What documentation and records are implied by Baldrige Award criteria?
- How can a documentation COE implement TQM?

At a seminar on the ISO 9000 series of quality system standards, the facilitator asked participants to identify their number one obstacle to becoming registered. Greater than 90 percent said documentation. According to the 1880 respondents of a 1996 survey of ISO 9000-registered firms, conducted by Irwin Professional Publishing and Dun & Bradstreet Information Services, "the greatest barriers to achieving registration were document development (57.9 percent) and procedure creation (41.0 percent) ("ISO 9000 for Quality's Sake" 1996).

Every major quality initiative (for example, ISO 9000 standards and the Baldrige Award) requires or implies documentation to communicate, control, monitor, or evaluate quality. Documentation serves as a keeper of process decisions. Its role is to provide guidance for consistent ways of operating. It enables employees to learn and be reminded of acceptable ways to fulfill work assignments. Documentation also can be a diagnostic tool that helps organizations target priorities for improving processes.

Documentation can demonstrate compliance with stated requirements or criteria. For ISO 9000, for example, effective quality policies, operating procedures, work instructions, and other documentation can convince auditors that processes are in place. For the Baldrige Award, documentation can show examiners that an organization delivers performance excellence. Other quality standards, regulations, and requirements—such as QS-9000, the FDA, and military specifications—demand accurate and current documentation to affirm safety, purity, protection, durability, and other attributes. World-class organizations can settle for nothing less than documentation that fulfills its purpose, yet is cost-effective, fast, and responsive to organizational and market change. To illustrate the role of documentation in quality initiatives, this section presents an overview of each of two quality initiatives, their documentation requirements or implications, and how TQM relates to a documentation function. The solutions are the same as for other Nimble Documentation®: a zero base; hierarchy, structure, format, and style that facilitate access and minimize resource consumption; standardized processes; and measured continuous improvement.

A. ISO 9000

ISO 9000 is a series of standards for quality management and quality assurance that apply to design, development, production, installation, and service. The series grew from the International Organization for Standardization started in Geneva, Switzerland, in 1946. (Although some writers attribute the term *ISO* to an acronym for the Swiss organization, most trace *ISO* to the Greek word *isos,* which, loosely translated, means *equal* or *consistent.*) In the two years prior to September 1995, the number of companies worldwide registered to ISO 9000 grew from about 48,000 to about 113,000. In the United States, the proportion has remained at about 6 or 7 percent of companies worldwide, or more than 7000 companies as of September 1995. Conservative estimates place newly registered U.S. companies at more than 300 each month.

Why are organizations putting so much time, energy, and resources into becoming ISO registered? Mostly, to gain six major benefits.

• Customer satisfaction

- Access to global markets

- Marketing

- Reduced costs and time

- Perceived quality

- Heightened staff morale

A supplier's customers may demand ISO 9000 registration, especially if the customer itself has achieved registration. Even agencies of the U.S. government, such as the National Aeronautics and Space Administration (NASA), are asking suppliers to be registered. ISO 9000 registration is mandatory for many European companies, stemming from European Union demands. To compete, other major traders in world commerce have begun to do the same. Splashy brochures and giveaways at trade shows and building banners proclaim ISO 9000 registration to attract business. For example, at a recent food technology and equipment convention in Portland, Oregon, several companies had stickers on their marketing materials and displayed congratulatory signs for their ISO 9000 registration. Several sales representatives at the convention said their companies may seek registration just because their competitors have.

The discipline required of quality management and operating processes can lead to greater efficiency and can save organizations time and dollars. Rework, waste, confusion, and inconsistencies all generate needless expense. Although ISO 9000 registration is not an assurance of quality products or services, this seal of approval gives that impression (and product and service quality nearly always improves with ISO 9000 assessment and registration). Most organizations form teams to help them achieve ISO registration. The common goal, the camaraderie, being listened to and paid attention to, knowing how to do a job, and training—all these elements of ISO 9000 teams—tend to contribute to a more satisfied and productive workforce.

The ISO 9000 series includes three standards: ISO 9001, 9002, and 9003. ISO 9001 is comprised of 20 sections corresponding to major quality system processes. ISO 9002 addresses all the sections of ISO 9001, except design control; this standard is appropriate for organizations that have a full range of quality system processes but are not involved in design. ISO 9003 includes 12 of the sections covered by ISO 9001; it is the least comprehensive standard of the series and applies mostly to organizations that focus primarily on testing and inspection. ISO 9003 does not address contract review, purchasing, control of customer-supplied product, process control, corrective and preventive action, internal quality audits, or servicing. The 20 sections of ISO 9001 are

1. Management responsibility
2. Quality system
3. Contract review
4. Design control
5. Document and data control
6. Purchasing
7. Control of customer-supplied product
8. Product identification and traceability
9. Process control
10. Inspection and testing
11. Control of inspection, measuring, and test equipment
12. Inspection and test status
13. Control of nonconforming product
14. Corrective and preventive action
15. Handling, storage, packaging, preservation, and delivery
16. Control of quality records
17. Internal quality audits
18. Training
19. Servicing
20. Statistical techniques

Where does the ISO 9000 series fit in the family of quality efforts? Is it just another quality initiative? Does an organization abandon current quality standards to embrace ISO 9000? Does it discard plans to seek the Baldrige Award?

Seeking either quality initiative usually leads to the same result: improved quality. And several clauses link the two initiatives. The Baldrige Award, however, is a single point. Once it is given, it's given. Further, the Baldrige Award means more to U.S. customers than to other nations. Additional features distinguish the two quality initiatives; however, both sets of criteria require or imply documentation to support processes. Figure 6.1 shows the ISO 9000 series of standards in a continuum of quality initiatives from no

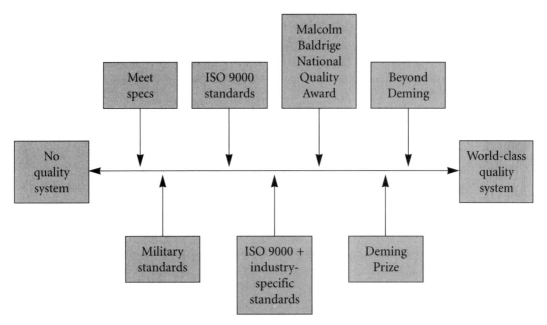

Source: John Kerr, *An Insider's Guide to ISO 9000,* n.d. Newport Beach, Calif.: IMPAC Integrated Systems, Inc. Used with permission.

Figure 6.1. A continuum of quality initiatives.

quality system to a world-class quality system. Documentation for the Baldrige Award is addressed in greater detail later in this chapter.

What are the documentation requirements of the ISO 9000 series standards? Each standard in the ISO 9000 series requires a supplier to define and document its quality policy. Individual sections of the standards specify documented procedures and records. To achieve ISO 9000 registration, most organizations develop a quality system manual as their first tier documentation. This manual communicates the organization's philosophy of and commitment to quality. Typically, organizations develop a second tier of operating procedures that implement the quality policy and define activities or processes. A third tier may include work instructions, that is, steps on using equipment, conducting transactions, and similar detailed guidance.

The most nimble quality system manuals are organized according to ISO 9000 clauses and seldom include more than 20 pages. Manuals that combine quality policy with operating procedures, naturally, will be longer. Some organizations merge operating procedures with work instructions in one manual. The level of detail in the documentation depends on the experience and skills of employees and the complexity of the process. No specification in the ISO 9000 standards dictates the hierarchy, structure, or format of required documentation. However, a common hierarchy is shown in Figure 6.2.

Commonly, the first tier quality system manual refers to each clause of the standard (20 clauses for ISO 9001) by clause number. For example, the organization's quality policy statement, signed by a senior executive, is placed in the quality system manual under the heading *4.1.1 Quality Policy.* Similarly, the kind of information contained in purchase orders and other purchasing documents is defined in the quality system manual under *4.6.6 Purchasing Data.* Where a lower-tier document details processes of the quality system required according to the ISO 9000 standard, that document is noted in the quality system manual. For example, in the quality system manual under *4.8 Product Identification and Traceability,* a paragraph refers by number and name to the company's traceability operating procedure. For company XXX, the operating procedure reference might be *XXXP 4-0 Product Traceability.* Depending on the company's quality system documentation hierarchy, structure, and format, work instructions may be referenced in a related operating

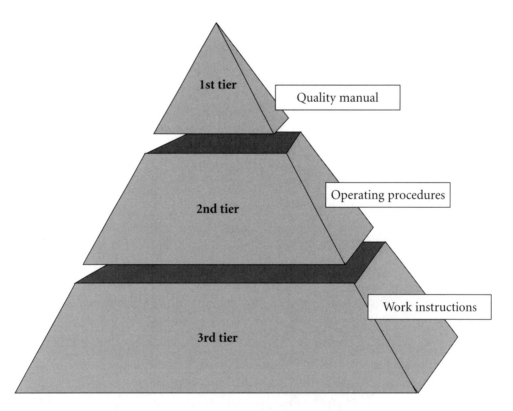

Figure 6.2. Common hierarchy for ISO 9000-compliant documentation.

procedure. The most user-friendly documentation systems number related documents, or their parts, similarly. For example, a work instruction for receiving product identification is numbered *XXXWI 4-0 A Receiving Product Identification* (see Chapter 3).

ISO 9000 requirements also specify records and data for control and verification. One definition of documentation is *recorded information.* And records, for many, mean *recorded evidence or proof.* The definitions of documentation and records overlap. The standards, however, are clear on requiring both. Forms are information templates that, completed, can serve as records, for example, evidence of employee training. Captured data, such as measurements driven by software-managed machinery, can also serve as records.

Every ISO 9000 standard specifies documentation or records. Many clauses spell out both. Table 6.1 shows ISO 9001 clauses that specify documentation and records. Typical placement for documenting how a company meets the requirements is shown in parentheses; however, the best documentation placement for a given company depends on many factors, including the number of documentation tiers, complexity of product or service, and experience and skill of personnel. Because the word *procedures* without the modifier *documented* is specified repeatedly in this standard, no attempt was made to identify individual clauses that could be fulfilled by *documented* procedures, unless specified that way by the standard. However, documented procedures or other publications (hard copy or electronic) typically are used to demonstrate and communicate the information that can fulfill these requirements. This chart generally omits reference to work instructions as typical documentation placement because companies vary widely in the scope and volume of work instructions needed for their processes. The term *procedures* rather than *procedure* is used when more than one operating procedure is customary; however, the number of related procedures varies from company to company and site to site.

Applying the principles of zero-based documentation to ISO 9000 requirements and a mind-set of continuous improvement can yield some streamlined solutions. For example, a quality system improvement team at a credit monitoring and reporting service recently used a combined training plan and record. The hybrid document fulfills two requirements of ISO 9001 section 4.18 Training: (1) identification of training needs and (2) training record. Figure 6.3 shows how the company's Individual Training Plan and Record lets supervisors and employees identify both required and elective

Table 6.1. ISO 9001 clauses that specify documentation or records.

Note: Parentheses indicate typical means of fulfilling the documentation requirement. Plural *Operating procedures* means more than one document typically is published to fulfill the requirement.

Number	Section and Clause	Documentation Requirement or Implication	Records Requirement
4.1	**MANAGEMENT RESPONSIBILITY**		
4.1.1	**Quality policy**	Quality policy, including objectives and commitment to quality. (Quality system manual)	
4.1.2.1	**Responsibility and authority**	Documented responsibility, authority, and the interrelation of personnel who manage, perform, and verify work affecting quality. (Organization chart in quality manual, statements of responsibilities, job descriptions or work instructions for quality function personnel)	Responsibility and authority of personnel who record problems relating to the product, process, and quality system. (Job descriptions or work instructions for quality function personnel for responsibility and authority; forms for records)
4.1.3	**Management review**		Records of management reviews. (Meeting minutes)
4.2	**QUALITY SYSTEM**		
4.2.1	**General**	Quality system manual, inclusion of or references to operating procedures, and outlined documentation structure	
4.2.2	**Quality system procedures**	(Operating procedure)	
4.2.3	**Quality planning**	Documented ways quality requirements will be met. Documented quality planning. (Quality system manual defined as primary quality plan)	Consideration to identification and preparation of quality records. (Operating procedures specify required records; forms for records)
4.3	**CONTRACT REVIEW**		
4.3.1	**General**	Documented procedure includes contract review and its coordination. (Operating procedure)	
4.3.2	**Review**	Documented requirements	
4.3.4	**Records**		Records of contract reviews. (Forms)

Table 6.1. *Continued.*

Number	Section and Clause	Documentation Requirement or Implication	Records Requirement
4.4	**DESIGN CONTROL**		
4.4.1	**General**	Documented procedures to control and verify product design. (Operating procedure)	
4.4.2	**Design and development planning**		Plans for each design and development activity
4.4.3	**Organizational and technical interfaces**	Documented information on interfaces	
4.4.4	**Design input**	Documented requirements relating to the product, including statutes and regulations	
4.4.5	**Design output**	Documented design output	
4.4.6	**Design review**	Formal documented reviews of design results	Records of design reviews. (Forms)
4.4.7	**Design verification**		Records of design-verification measures. (Forms)
4.4.9	**Design changes**	Documented design changes	
4.5	**DOCUMENT AND DATA CONTROL**		
4.5.1	**General**	(Operating procedure)	
4.5.2	**Document and data approval and issue**	Reviewed and approved documents and data. Established document control procedure. (Operating procedure)	
4.5.3	**Document and data changes**	Reviewed, approved, and identified changes to documents and data	
4.6	**PURCHASING**		
4.6.1	**General**	(Operating procedure)	
4.6.2	**Evaluation of subcontractors**		Quality audit reports or quality records of subcontractors' previously demonstrated capability and performance. Quality records of acceptable subcontractors. (Forms, including checklists)

Table 6.1. *Continued.*

Number	Section and Clause	Documentation Requirement or Implication	Records Requirement
4.6.3	**Purchasing data**	Reviewed and approved purchasing documents	
4.6.4.1	**Supplier verification at subcontractor's premises**	Specified verification arrangements and method of product release	
4.7	**CONTROL OF CONSUMER-SUPPLIED PRODUCT**	Documented procedures for control verification, storage, and maintenance of customer-supplied product. (Operating procedures)	Records of products lost, damaged, or otherwise unsuitable for use
4.8	**PRODUCT IDENTIFICATION AND TRACEABILITY**	Where appropriate, documented procedures for identifying the product from receipt and during all stages of production, delivery, and installation. (Operating procedures) Documented procedures for unique identification of individual product or batches. (Operating procedure)	Records of identification. (Forms or log books)
4.9	**PROCESS CONTROL**	Documented procedures to define the manner of production, installation, and servicing, and compliance with reference standards/codes, quality plans, or procedures. (Operating procedures) Documented workmanship criteria	Records for processes, equipment, and personnel
4.10	**INSPECTION AND TESTING**		
4.10.1	**General**	Documented procedures for inspection and testing activities. (Operating procedures)	Inspection and testing records detailed in quality plan or operating procedures. (Forms or log books)
4.10.2.1	**[Paragraph 1]**	Verified requirements according to quality plan or operating procedure	
4.10.2.2	**[Paragraph 2]**		Recorded evidence of conformance. (Forms or log books)

Table 6.1. *Continued.*

Number	Section and Clause	Documentation Requirement or Implication	Records Requirement
4.10.2.3	[Paragraph 3]		Records of incoming product released for urgent production prior to verification. (Forms or log books)
4.10.3	**In-process inspection and testing**	Inspected and tested product according to quality plan or operating procedure	
4.10.4	**Final inspection and testing**	Final inspection and testing according to quality plan or operating procedure	
4.11	**CONTROL OF INSPECTION, MEASURING, AND TEST EQUIPMENT**		
4.11.1	**General**	Documented procedures to control, calibrate, and maintain inspection, measuring, and test equipment, including test software. (Operating procedures)	Records of extent and frequency of checks. (Log books and tags)
4.11.2	**Control procedure**	Where no internationally or nationally recognized standards exist, documented basis for calibration. Documented validity of previous inspection and test results when inspection, measuring, and test equipment found to be out of calibration	Calibration records.
4.12	**INSPECTION AND TEST STATUS**	Identification of inspection and test status according to quality plan or operating procedure	
4.13	**CONTROL OF NONCONFORMING PRODUCT**		
4.13.1	**General**	Documented procedures to ensure that nonconforming product is not used or installed unintentionally. (Operating procedure) (Work instructions for disposition of nonconforming product)	

Table 6.1. *Continued.*

Number	Section and Clause	Documentation Requirement or Implication	Records Requirement
4.13.2	**Review and disposition of nonconforming product**	Documented procedures for reviewing nonconforming product. (Operating procedure) Repaired or reworked product reinspected according to quality plan or procedure	Records of nonconformities and repairs
4.14	**CORRECTIVE AND PREVENTIVE ACTION**		
4.14.1	**General**	Documented procedures for implementing corrective and preventive action. (Operating procedures) Implemented and recorded changes to procedures resulting from corrective and preventive action	Records of procedure changes resulting from corrective and preventive action
4.14.3	**Preventive action**		Quality records, service reports, and customer complaints included in preventive action procedures
4.15	**HANDLING, STORAGE, PACKAGING, PRESERVATION, AND DELIVERY**		
4.15.1	**General**	Documented procedures for handling, storing, packaging, preserving, and delivering product. (Operating procedures)	
4.16	**CONTROL OF QUALITY RECORDS**	Documented procedures for identifying, collecting, indexing, accessing, filing, storing, maintaining, and disposition of quality records. (Operating procedures)	Quality records, including subcontractors', and retention times
4.17	**INTERNAL QUALITY AUDITS**	Documented procedures for planning and implementing internal quality audits. (Operating procedure)	Records of audit results and follow-up activities. (Forms)
4.18	**TRAINING**	Documented procedures for identifying training needs and for training personnel. (Operating procedure)	Training records. (Forms)

Table 6.1. *Continued.*

Number	Section and Clause	Documentation Requirement or Implication	Records Requirement
4.19	SERVICING	Documented procedures for performing, verifying, and reporting that servicing meets specified requirements. (Operating procedures)	
4.20	STATISTICAL TECHNIQUES		
4.20.2	Procedures	Documented procedures to implement and control the application of statistical techniques. (Operating procedure)	

training needs. Instructions are printed directly on the form, which is numbered corresponding to the ISO 9001 clause. The revision date is printed on the form, as well. A related operating procedure only references, but doesn't duplicate, the form. Filed in each employee's personnel file, the form also becomes a record of completed training. Only one document is processed and maintained. Plenty of other opportunities, like this one, exist for translating ISO requirements into Nimble Documentation®.

Organizations seeking registration to one of the ISO 9000 series standards are wise to first assess their existing quality system processes and corresponding documentation. Trained internal personnel or consultants can perform a preliminary gap analysis to match processes and documentation, including records, against the standards. Findings generated by the analysis should specify any major and minor nonconformities in both processes and documentation. Recommendations should be specific.

For more information on ISO 9000 series requirements, see Resources or browse the web. The American Society for Quality (ASQ) maintains a web site at http://www.asq.org, where you can link to other web sites for ISO 9000 information. ASQ's monthly magazine, *Quality Progress*, frequently includes articles about ISO 9000.

Figure 6.4 places the quality initiative's documentation requirements in perspective.

Individual Training Plan and Record

Employee name: _____ Employee number: _____

              Last   First   Middle initial

Education, training, or certification	Required	Elective (Check one)	Date required	Date completed
Example: B.S. Finance		✔		6/15/90
Example: WCQMS Employee Awareness	✔		7/31/96	7/30/96

Instructions:
For required training, enter the name of the training, check the *Required* box, and enter the date by which training needs to be completed. After training is completed, enter the date training was completed.
For elective training, enter the name of the training, check the *Elective* box, and enter the date training was completed.

WXY Form 18 Rev. 09/12/96

Figure 6.3. Individual training plan and record.

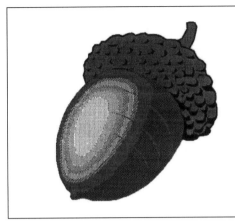

- If it moves, **train** it!

- If it doesn't move, **calibrate** it!

- If it isn't **documented,** it doesn't exist!

- If it isn't **authorized,** it didn't happen!

Text from Ann Niese, ISO 9000 Management and Archive Corporation

Source: Ann Niese, course notes, *Implementing ISO 9000,* presented at California State University, Long Beach, Calif. May 6–20, 1995. Used with permission.

Figure 6.4. ISO 9000 in a nutshell.

B. The Baldrige Award

John Kerr, in "But Is It Better Than Baldrige?" presents four distinctions between the ISO 9000 series of quality system standards and the Baldrige Award.

1. ISO is not anyone's personal philosophy; it's an internationally ratified, bona fide *standard.*

2. ISO 9000 is easy to understand. "People see the short-term value in getting organized," says consultant Bob Bowen.

3. Where the Baldrige Award preoccupies contestants with goal-setting, ISO 9000 certification is the tool that opens the door to continuous improvement practices.

4. The Baldrige Award uses self-assessment, with a board of examiners screening for best practices. With ISO 9000, you document your process and the assessors come in to see if you've applied your documentation.

On the cover of the 1997 Baldrige Award criteria, U.S. President Bill Clinton refers to the award in national marketing terms.

> *The United States is the most competitive nation in the world. Quality is a key to retaining that title. The Malcolm Baldrige*

National Quality Award is helping U.S. companies satisfy cus-
tomers and improve overall company performance and capa-
bilities. (National Institute of Standards and Technology
1997)

In the same publication are these words from Michael Kantor, U.S.
Secretary of Commerce.

The Malcolm Baldrige National Quality Award Program has
had a profound influence on increasing U.S. competitiveness
and heightening our awareness to the challenges we face in a
global economy. (National Institute of Standards and Technology
1997)

Established by Public Law 100-107, the Malcolm Baldrige National
Quality Improvement Act of 1987 was signed by President Ronald Reagan.
Its purposes were to promote the awareness of quality excellence, to recognize quality achievement of U.S. companies, and to publicize successful
quality strategies. It is given annually to a manufacturing company, or
subsidiary; service company, or subsidiary; and small business. Where
ISO 9000 registration verifies a *company's* consistent, reliable quality system, the Baldrige Award advertises a *nation's* business quality as well as
companies'. The Baldrige Award specifically excludes government agencies,
not-for-profit organizations, trade associations, and professional societies
from eligibility.

The award is conferred through a four-stage process. First, organizations
submit a comprehensive application, which is reviewed and evaluated by a
board of examiners. The application summarizes the company's practices
and performance. Applications that score well in the first stage are subjected
to a consensus review and evaluation. At the third stage, examiners visit the
sites of applicants that score well in stage two. At stage four, a panel of judges
review applications and recommend candidate award recipients to the
Secretary of Commerce. After it is determined that an applicant will not
move to the next stage of consideration, each applicant receives a feedback
report. Prepared by the board of examiners, the reports target key gaps, reinforce company strengths, and help applicants learn new and better ways to
evaluate suppliers, customers, partners, and even competitors.

Unlike ISO 9000 standards, the Baldrige Award's seven examination
criteria only indirectly refer to documentation. For example, they require

demonstration that a company's operational requirements address regulatory and other legal requirements. The company must show excellence through its action plans. It must show how the company obtains objective and reliable information on customer satisfaction. Its information and data must support key business operations and business strategy. Demonstration of a company's performance management can be translated into documentation.

The zero-based approach and measured improvement features of Nimble Documentation®, on the other hand, correspond directly to the Baldrige Award criteria. Firms or departments that provide documentation (for instance, technical editing and word processing businesses or S&P functions), could benefit from the Baldrige Award criteria to evaluate and improve their own processes. Section 2.2, Company Strategy, for example, examines how key strategic planning requirements translate into effective performance management and include performance requirements and measures. Consider documentation metrics to fulfill these criteria such as customer satisfaction, zero defects, currentness, cycle time, volume, and cost. These indicators, discussed in Chapter 5, could contribute to an effective performance management system for a documentation COE (see Chapter 9) or other Nimble Documentation® function. The Baldrige Award criteria category 5.0, Human Resource Development and Management, focuses on how a workforce is enabled to develop and use its full potential and how it aligns with performance objectives. Compare this category to COE self-directed team goals and performance, accountability, and evaluation. Each addresses a working environment conducive to full participation. Or look at the Baldrige Award criteria category 6.0 Process Management. This category examines customer-focused design, product, and service delivery processes. The foundation of zero-based documentation is its sources of need, including customers. The litmus test questions ask about customers' needs (see Chapter 2). Baldrige award categories 6.2 and 6.3 address continuous improvement (Chapter 5). The Baldrige Award category 7.0 is Business Results; consider the documentation cost model (Chapter 5). Performance management is the heart of the Baldrige Award. It is also the heart of Nimble Documentation® processes.

Following are the seven Baldrige Award criteria categories.

1.0 Leadership

2.0 Strategic planning

3.0   Customer and market focus

4.0   Information and analysis

5.0   Human resource development and management

6.0   Process management

7.0   Business results

Each criterion requires some form of documentation, or evidence or record of conformity. Information and data from many sources (for example, from employees and customers) thread through the criteria. At the least, applicants for the award need to prepare extensive documentation to be reviewed by a board of examiners.

Table 6.2 shows a few Baldrige Award criteria categories as examples of documentation requirements or implications for written evidence. Common placement for documenting a company's compliance with the criteria is shown in parentheses; however, companies use a variety of formats to document Baldrige Award criteria, including policies and practices, annual reports, and formal plans.

C. Total Quality Management

Some say the *T* in *total quality management* really stands for *transformation.* A way to think of TQM is permeating the achievement of quality purposefully, rather than accidentally, through the pores of an organization. But, unlike the ISO 9000 series of standards, TQM is not a model. It is a philosophy. TQM continues where ISO 9000 leaves off. David S. Huyink, past chair of the ISO 9000 Quality Consortium, sees ISO 9000 as "a model with an embedded philosophy" and TQM as a "philosophy that can be expressed through a model such as the Malcolm Baldrige National Quality Award criteria" (1996, 615).

TQM focuses on continuously providing products that meet customer expectations at competitive prices—it is built on a quality foundation but sports a business spin.

John J. Hudiburg, former chairman and chief executive officer of Florida Power and Light, describes three most important factors for successful TQM.

> *First is a strong, visible, and consistent commitment by top management. This needs to be constantly emphasized and*

Table 6.2. Examples of Baldrige Award criteria and documentation requirements and implications.

Item	Heading	Documentation Requirements
1.2	**Company Responsibility and Citizenship**	How the company addresses the current and potential impacts on society. (Policies or practices)
2.1	**Strategy Development Process**	How the company sets strategic directions for its competitive position, and how strategy development leads to an action plan. (Plans)
3.2	**Customer Satisfaction and Relationship Enhancement**	How the company provides information to enable customers to seek assistance, conduct business, and voice complaints. (Practices)
4.1	**Selection and Use of Information and Data**	Selection, management, and use of information and data to improve the company's overall performance.
4.2	**Selection and Use of Comparisons and Information and Data**	Comparative information and data include benchmarking and competitive comparisons.
4.3	**Analysis and Review of Company Performance**	How performance data are integrated and analyzed to assess overall company performance in key areas. (Practices)
5.2	**Employee Education, Training, and Development**	How the company's education and training address key company plans and needs. (Objectives and practices)
5.3	**Employee Well-Being and Satisfaction**	How the company maintains a work environment that supports employee well-being, satisfaction, and motivation. (Practices and outlines)
6.1	**Management of Product and Service Processes**	How new, significantly modified, and customized products and services are designed. (Practices)
7.4	**Supplier and Partner Results**	Results of supplier and partner performance. (Data)

reinforced as a key success factor for the company. Second is a strong commitment to education and training of all employees. And last, it must be profoundly understood that there has to be a concrete system in place to make it happen, a systematic way of encouraging all employees to do their best. (Hudiburg 1991, 185)

Whereas ISO 9000 clauses specifically require quality system documentation for compliance, the Baldrige Award criteria imply documentation, primarily in the shape of plans and records, and other information formats, and as evidence of meeting the criteria. TQM, however, does not indicate documentation at all.

TQM is addressed in this book not as a requirement or implication *of* documentation, but rather as a way an organization *does* documentation. Consider that TQM philosophy mirrors the elements of a documentation COE, as shown here.

Checklist 6.1: Total Quality Managed Documentation Function
☐ Plans and actions responsive to needs
☐ Focus on strategic business goals
☐ Leadership committed to managed change
☐ Excellence throughout the organization
☐ All employees participate
☐ Employees skilled in examining and improving processes continuously
☐ Optimum performance from everyone
☐ Highly trained employees
☐ Cross-functional teams

- All plans and actions are responsive to demonstrated needs, including customers'.
- Focus is on strategic business goals.
- Leadership is committed to managed change.
- Excellence is built into every aspect of the organization.
- All employees participate.
- Employees are skilled in examining and improving processes continuously.
- Optimum performance is expected from every department and every employee.
- Employees are highly trained.
- Cross-functional teams are important.

From a corporate S&P department to a word processing and editing firm to a documentation contractor, TQM means quality for a documentation business. Consider each of the elements of TQM in terms of a documentation COE.

All plans and actions are responsive to demonstrated needs, including customers'. Customer service feedback sheets, focus group meetings with document owners to plan the format of procedures, the litmus test for streamlining documentation systems, improving uploading cycle time to meet managers' requirements—each of these are examples of TQM applied to a documentation function.

Focus is on strategic business goals. Flowing down company goals to function, team, and individual objectives points performance in the right direction.

Leadership is committed to managed change. Management supports transforming an organization into self-directed teams and provides resources for their success.

Excellence is built into every aspect of the organization. Examples include nonglare lighting, zero-defects forms, current bulletins, and lightning turnaround time for uploading.

All employees participate. The secretary becomes the leader of the team to overhaul organization charts, a plaque is awarded for 100 percent participation in continuous measurable improvement training.

Employees are skilled in examining and improving processes continuously. Staff members learn how to flowchart, establish and maintain metrics, and use fishbones for problem solving—*living* improvement.

Optimum performance is expected from every department and every employee. Text processors are accountable for proofreading their work, and managers volunteer for 180-degree performance evaluations to learn how to listen better.

Employees are highly trained. Uploaders become network certified to administer LANs, analysts train on improved document management software, and text processors learn to use stylesheets and macros.

Cross-functional teams are important. The approval authority team brings in representatives of finance, legal, HR, and other functions to improve the approval authority system.

Despite the fact that TQM does not specify or imply documentation, the TQM model mirrors the elements of a documentation COE and can be applied to reinforce introduction of quality improvement processes.

CHAPTER 7

Other Applications

Solutions presented in this chapter address documentation challenges such as

- Why a disclaimer belongs in an employee handbook
- How to make a user manual people-friendly
- Why measured improvement is important for safety program documentation
- How to keep ISO 14001 documentation lean
- What other documentation applications can benefit from the nimble approach

The basic elements of Nimble Documentation®—meeting customers' requirements and other sources of need, helping organizations respond quickly to changing market and workplace conditions, and maintaining only documentation that fulfills a demonstrated need—apply very well to a wide variety of documentation for world-class organizations. This chapter shows how the approach works for employee handbooks, user manuals, safety program documentation, and ISO 14001 requirements. The chapter also briefly describes the approach's value to other applications.

A. Employee Handbooks

Say *employee handbook* and what comes to mind? For many, a picture emerges of bureaucratic policies, rules, and procedures. Small business owners who left larger companies because they were weary of all the regulations may be reluctant to establish employee rules. Managers of other organizations may see written policies as invitations for employee abuse. It doesn't have to be that way. In fact, some policies are legally required, such as preventing sexual harassment and discrimination. Further, spelling out workplace guidance sets a good foundation for growth. New companies that can get by without much formal direction find employees bumping into one another when the work population soars. They yell "unfair" when employees are treated differently by different supervisors. They yell "unfair" louder to regulatory agencies and courts. Written policies can prevent misunderstandings, confusion, and duplicated effort, and they can reduce exposure to legal challenges and judgments. Employee handbooks allow employees to concentrate on core business. But how do the features of Nimble Documentation® apply to employee handbooks?

Start with customers. Ask Who are they? What do they want to know? What laws and contractual requirements translate into employee issues? What harm could come to the organization if a proposed document or piece of information were omitted? What harm could come if it were *included*? And, finally, ask How can an organization improve an existing handbook, for example, to lower costs, facilitate access, and keep information up to date?

These are the same basic questions to ask of quality management system manuals, operating procedures, forms, records, and other documentation. The answers to these questions, the litmus test of documentation plus inquiry into continuous process improvement, form the backbone of a world-class employee handbook.

Federal and state laws in the United States; national, provincial, and regional laws elsewhere; and municipal statutes dictate some of the information for employee handbooks. Workers compensation regulations and rules about smoking, alcohol, and drugs at the workplace all have a place in the handbooks. You will see work hours; vacation, attendance, and leave policies; disability and disciplinary procedures; codes of conduct; and insurance provisions. In some handbooks, policies are written for personal appearance, direct deposit banking, and performance evaluations. Not surprisingly, employee policies often stretch across the greater portion of comprehensive company policies and practices manuals. Companies that maintain data on specific handbook topics typically report that users research employee policies more than any other general set of topics.

A very large electronics firm recently was converting its hard copy manuals to an on-line information storage and retrieval system. During the testing phase, an improvement team was collecting information on the number of hits each on-line document received. The team intended to check each document against litmus test questions. If no one ever viewed a particular document, and communicating the policy in writing was not required by law or contract, the team considered omitting the policy from the new system. Every time a user looked at a screen, the system registered the view as a hit and compiled usage statistics on the document. Overwhelmingly, the most popular documents were employee policies. Workers wanted to know about benefits, but they also searched for information on layoffs, the company's performance appraisal rating system, and the policy prohibiting smoking in company buildings.

The same team recommended canceling an administrative guidebook and a supervisor's reference book, which included obsolete and duplicate employee policies. The company, which at the time was reorganizing and undergoing massive changes in the workforce and in its programs, decided the HR function could no longer keep the information in these books current. The function recognized the potential liability of obsolete and conflicting documentation, especially concerning employee benefits and procedures. Changes in personnel laws also contributed to the obsolescence. Perhaps no other area of documentation these days changes as frequently as employee policies.

Nimble Documentation® means information that is required or wanted, error-free, current, easy to access, responsive to changing conditions, and volume and cost conscious. The team delivered.

The recommendations in this book for user-friendly formats and styles (Chapter 3) and for a user manual index (hard copy) or search engine (on-line) apply to employee handbooks as well (see the User Manuals section [B] of this chapter).

Another consideration for an employee handbook is a disclaimer. When is a contract not a contract? The answer is when it says so. World-class organizations avoid spending valuable resources on defending themselves. Attorney Susan K. Krell of Jackson, Lewis, Schnitzler & Krupman, Hartford, Conn., writes in *The Personnel Law Update* (1995) about an employee who successfully sued a company claiming that the company handbook was an "implied contract" that conferred specific rights that the company violated.

This is not the first time a company has found itself incurring unintended liability because of its policies and practices manual. That handy book can lead to big headaches if it's not worded properly. Krell suggests including a prominent disclaimer that states the handbook or manual is *not* a contract, that it is provided only for informational purposes, and that the information may be revised at any time at the sole discretion of the company.

One disclaimer that is brief and clear is published by Hughes Aircraft Company in its on-line Company Policies and Practices Manual.

> *The policies, practices, and procedures set forth in this Company Policies and Practices Manual are guidelines for supervision. They are not intended to confer contractual rights of any kind upon any employee, or to create contractual obligations of any kind for the Company. The Company may revise, delete, or supplement any policy, practice, or procedure in this Company Policies and Practices Manual at any time in its sole discretion. (Hughes Aircraft Company, Company Policies and Practices Manual, 1996. Reprinted by permission.)*

A disclaimer, a company may find, is more important for an employee handbook, or employee policies in a comprehensive manual, than in any other kind of business documentation.

To get a head start on developing an employee handbook, consider readily available resources. Software catalogs and retailers routinely advertise several employee handbooks available on disk. Libraries and book shops carry sample hard copy manuals. Also, firms such as the Independent Small Business Employers of America publish hard copy options for handbooks along with a customizable floppy disk. Any of these aids can be a catalyst for an organization that is having difficulty generating an employee handbook (see Resources). The most challenging and time-consuming part of the effort, however, is customizing these documents, which often means structuring and facilitating interviews or focus groups with key personnel. In any case, it is advisable to seek professional legal advice before publishing an employee handbook.

B. User Manuals

User manuals are the first thing we see when we unpack a new computer or VCR, but the last thing we turn to when we are in trouble. What is it about them that makes user manuals so intimidating?

The best ones reduce users' frustrations—and time responding to SOS calls, faxes, and mail. Can user manuals serve as goodwill ambassadors? It's possible.

Similar questions posed for employee handbooks guide the development of user manuals along the Nimble Documentation® path. Who are the customers? What do they want to know? What harm could come if a proposed piece of information or step were omitted? What harm could come if it were included? How can an organization improve an existing user manual, for example, to reduce costs, facilitate access, and keep information current with changing technology?

Informal correspondence with many users over the years indicates the benefits of the following features; however, the best way to create a good user manual is to get customers' direct feedback. How do you do that? One way is to maintain help line databases. Document trouble calls and maintain statistics to surface rough spots. Discover the kind of problems that plague users again and again. Then, draft a revised manual to clarify the problem areas. Pilot the draft with lay users (nontechnical personnel). Eliminate unnecessary instructions that might distract readers and contribute to a manual's intimidating bulkiness.

Include tips on undoing steps, particularly for long sequences of instruction. "Undo" instructions are a godsend. All humans at least occasionally press the wrong key or overlook a step. Help users undo missteps. Include call-out boxes, marginal notes, and other highlighted instructions. The true story of the *any* key teaches us not to assume anything (see Chapter 2).

Modular or play script formats suit user manuals well for several reasons. One, step-by-step instructions written in these formats are easy to follow, and two, *if-then* decision points stand out (see Chapter 3). It doesn't hurt that these formats also project a high-tech image. Graphics, especially screen captures, help users relate instructions printed in the manual to what they see on their monitors.

If a prize were awarded to documentation that frustrates users, it would have to go to inadequate indexes. How many times has each of us looked in a user manual for help, known the instructions we needed were in there because we found them before, and still could not locate the information we needed!

If you are responsible for writing a user manual, test drive the draft index with people who are unfamiliar with the product. Gather all the terms that they could use to look up the same information. Here is a case in point. At least six different terms are used for logging off, depending on the operating system and application: *bye, end, exit, logout, logoff,* and *quit.*

Include synonyms, terms that are more general, and more specific words. Don't be afraid of redundancy. Remember that few people read an index like a novel. They read only the entries they need. For example, include *search* as well as *find, preferences* as well as *options.* List subheadings by themselves as well as under other terms. For example, list *smart quotes* as an individual entry as well as *smart* indented under *quotes.*

Be generous with cross references. And remember to beef up the on-line help function, which is just an index in electronic clothing. For some applications, an on-line help function works well. For others, users need to compare instructions with the screen in front of them; therefore, hard copy instructions (or a second computer) are best. Users can also print help line function screens, but unbound sheets of paper often get discarded or lost and need to be reprinted.

Finding information in a well-equipped user manual can be faster than getting a colleague's response to a user's voice mail message or a technical support person's live voice.

C. Safety Programs

Like employee handbooks and user manuals, documentation for safety programs benefits from the nimble approach. In this case, legal requirements serve as some of the customers, because they must be satisfied to maintain an organization's good business health. Other customer requirements may be contractual; for example, a construction company may be obligated by written agreement to provide safety training to workers at a building site. Also, employees are customers because they use procedures manuals, training records, and other safety program documentation.

Some states, such as California, require companies to establish and maintain programs to ensure a safe and healthy environment for their employees. An injury and illness prevention program that complies with the California Codes of Regulations specifies documentation components, such as a code of safe practices, including supervisor and employee responsibilities, working conditions, and protective equipment; records of formal inspections to verify compliance with the codes; records of workplace-related accident, near-miss, and illness investigations and corrective action; and employee training records.

Nimble Documentation® for safety programs, like other policies, practices, and procedures, adopts a zero-based approach (see Chapter 2). Only information required by law, contract, or prudent business practice is included.

Only information that can harm an organization if omitted is documented. Safety program records are maintained and stored according to the specifications of an integrated records retention program. Documentation includes forms necessary to meet program requirements, such as accident investigation, employee safety suggestion, employee training, and hazard evaluation and abatement. Figures 7.1 and 7.2 present sample forms for a group safety training session and hazard evaluation and abatement, respectively. They were prepared for an educational agency.

The organization's approval authority system assigns responsibilities for the safety program, including establishing policy. For example, the program itself is approved by the highest level operations officer or designee. A safety coordinator verifies accident investigations and evaluates safety hazards and both employees and supervisors verify that employees have completed required safety training.

The plain vanilla text format (see Chapter 3) is common for safety manuals and usually is adequate and economical to write and maintain. Whatever format is adopted, step-by-step instructions for handling safety emergencies should be especially quick to access and easy to follow.

Measured improvement to an organization's safety program documentation could encompass some of the same elements as other documentation. Useful metrics include indicators of defect-free writing; currentness; processing time, which is particularly important for investigating and correcting workplace hazards and injuries; training; volume; and cost (see Chapter 5).

Because laws and regulations change, and organizations may restructure frequently, establishing and maintaining regularly scheduled safety documentation reviews are important. Speedy processing time for investigating and correcting problems prevents subsequent accidents, injuries, and illnesses. Metrics that capture processing time support improvement efforts objectively and eliminate sometimes divisive hearsay. Well-maintained and regularly reviewed safety training records provide feedback on employees who have been trained and those who need to be scheduled for training. Volume metrics tend to keep documentation trim. Finally, organizations that know the cost of their processes, including safety documentation, can investigate alternatives. For example, regularly measured costs allow an organization to compare the expense of preparing and revising documentation by internal documentation staff, by a safety function or department, by the general administrative function, or by an outside contractor (outsourcing). Without cost metrics, objective improvement decisions are hard to come by,

---

[LMN Logo]
Group Safety Training Session

Date of training: _____ Trainer: _____

Type of training: I & IP: _____ Hazard communication: _____

Training schedule: Initial: _____ Refresher: _____ New assignment: _____

The following employees have attended the training session indicated above. Training was conducted according to training procedure LMNP 17A. The signature of each employee verifies that he or she has attended this training session.

Employee name (please print)	Employee number	Employee signature
1.		
2.		
3.		
4.		
5.		
6.		
7.		
8.		
9.		
10.		
11.		
12.		
13.		
14.		
15.		

_____
Signature of safety trainer

LMN Form 17A Rev. 11/17/95

Figure 7.1. Group safety training session form.

[LMN Logo]

Hazard Evaluation and Abatement Form

Date of inspection: _____ Inspector: _____

Department: _____ Location: _____

General Observations

1. **Housekeeping**
   (   ) Acceptable   (   ) Corrective action needed   (   ) Not applicable

   _____

   _____

   _____

2. **Fire extinguishers**
   (   ) Acceptable   (   ) Corrective action needed   (   ) Not applicable

   _____

   _____

   _____

3. **First aid and emergency response equipment**
   (   ) Acceptable   (   ) Corrective action needed   (   ) Not applicable

   _____

   _____

   _____

4. **Electrical**
   (   ) Acceptable   (   ) Corrective action needed   (   ) Not applicable

   _____

   _____

   _____

Page 1 of 2
LMN Form 17B Rev. 12/4/95

Figure 7.2. Hazard evaluation and abatement form.

5. **Material handling and storage**
   (   ) Acceptable   (   ) Corrective action needed   (   ) Not applicable

   _____

   _____

   _____

6. **Equipment**
   (   ) Acceptable   (   ) Corrective action needed   (   ) Not applicable

   _____

   _____

   _____

7. **Exits**
   (   ) Acceptable   (   ) Corrective action needed   (   ) Not applicable

   _____

   _____

   _____

8. **Personal protective equipment**
   (   ) Acceptable   (   ) Corrective action needed   (   ) Not applicable

   _____

   _____

   _____

9. **Storage areas**
   (   ) Acceptable   (   ) Corrective action needed   (   ) Not applicable

   _____

   _____

   _____

Completed by: _____ Date: _____

Page 2 of 2
LMN Form 17B Rev. 12/4/95

Figure 7.2. *Continued.*

and organizations tend to keep the status quo—even if the status quo is needlessly expensive.

Features of nimble indexes for safety manuals, hard copy or on-line, are the same as for user manuals. For example, *glasses* should be listed as a stand-alone entry and should also be listed under *protective equipment,* under *eye care,* and as *safety glasses.*

D. ISO 14001

ISO 14001, a standard for environmental management systems, is another application whose documentation requirements and implications can benefit from the nimble approach. This section presents an overview of the standard, then addresses its documentation issues.

As communications technology continues to expand, the world continues to shrink. World-class companies are constantly finding better and faster ways to communicate and, as they march toward a global economy, more and more are finding it is just as easy to do business in Brussels as it is in Burbank. The problems crop up when companies want to do business in both Brussels *and* Burbank.

ISO 14001 was developed to provide a structure for environmental management that would be accepted globally and could be integrated with organizations' overall management activity. Another goal of the standard was to provide assurance that environmental performance would meet the many and sometimes confusing array of regulatory, audit, and other environmental management requirements. Creation of the standard has also been in response to public concern over industrial impact on both the local and world environment. The growing sentiment is that organizations should take responsibility for their own deeds.

With the potential to replace regional and national environmental requirements that impede international commerce, ISO 14001 also may reduce the costs associated with compliance with multiple systems—a particular benefit for multinational firms. The scope of ISO 14001 is broad, and international suppliers may feel pressure to comply.

ISO 14001 is similar to ISO 9001 in that both are comprehensive standards. Also like ISO 9000, the 14000 series includes guidelines. Prudent businesses are adopting the standard to reduce potential environmental liabilities before they become problems and are promoting awareness among employees of the connection between their jobs and environmental compliance.

ISO 14001 features six major environmental management system requirements.

1. General requirements

2. Environmental policy

3. Planning

4. Implementation and operation

5. Checking and corrective action

6. Management review

Documentation, as in the ISO 9000 series of standards and other quality initiatives, is a critical component of ISO 14001. Several clauses of the standard clearly specify documentation, such as *environmental objectives and targets; roles, responsibility, and authorities; information, in paper or electronic form, to (a) describe the core elements of the management system and their interaction and (b) provide direction to related documentation; and documented procedures* (ASQC, ISO, and ANSI 1996). Other ISO 14001 clauses imply documentation, or, at least, can be fulfilled through documented policies, procedures, and records (see Table 7.1). Documentation also can be a primary vehicle for promoting employee awareness of the system and for establishing a history of responsible environmental management.

Environmental management documentation may be integrated into an organization's standard management and operating policies and procedures or it may stand alone. Many processes that affect quality and are specified in quality system documentation also apply to environmental management. However, many organizations integrate their quality system documentation into standard management and operating policies and procedures. ISO 14001 does not specify how an organization meets its documentation requirements and should not justify more manuals if existing documentation can accommodate environmental management. In fact, the introduction to the standard itself addresses the option of complying with ISO 14001 requirements by adapting existing management system elements.

Forms can fulfill some of the records requirements of the standard (clause 4.5.3) and approval authority for environmental management transactions can meet structure and responsibility requirements (clause 4.4.1). Documentation functions may wish to pay particular attention to clauses 4.4.5, Document control, and 4.5.3, Records.

How do the features of Nimble Documentation® apply to ISO 14001? Their applicability is fundamentally the same as for company policies and

Table 7.1. ISO 14001 requirements and implications for documentation and records.

Note: The term *implied documentation* means documented procedures or other publications (hard copy or electronic) typically are used to demonstrate and communicate the information that can fulfill these requirements.

Number	Section and Clause	Documentation Requirement or Implication	Records Requirement
4.2	**ENVIRON-MENTAL POLICY**	Documented environmental policy.	
4.3	**PLANNING**		
4.3.1	**Environmental aspects**	[Implied documentation] Procedure to identify the environmental aspects of controlled activities, products, or services that can significantly impact the environment.	
4.3.2	**Legal and other requirements**	[Implied documentation] Procedure to identify legal and other environmental requirements.	
4.3.3	**Objectives and targets**	Documented environmental objectives and targets at every relevant function and level within the organization.	
4.4	**IMPLEMENTATION AND OPERATION**		
4.4.1	**Structure and responsibility**	Documented roles, responsibility, and authority.	
4.4.2	**Training, awareness and competence**	[Implied documentation] Procedures for importance of conformance, significant environmental impacts of work activities and benefits of improved performance, roles and responsibilities in achieving conformance, and potential consequences of nonconformance.	
4.4.3	**Communication**	[Implied documentation] Procedures for internal communication. Documented procedures for communication from external interested parties.	Recorded decisions on processes for external communication on its significant environmental aspects.

Table 7.1. *Continued.*

Number	Section and Clause	Documentation Requirement or Implication	Records Requirement
4.4.4	**Environmental management system documentation**	Information, in electronic or hard copy media, to • Describe core elements of the environmental management system and their interaction • Guide related documentation	
4.4.5	**Document control**	[Implied documentation] Procedures to control required documents to ensure they • Can be located • Are reviewed periodically, updated when needed, and approved by authorized personnel • Are available in current version at all locations where essential environmental management system activities are performed • Are promptly removed from use when no longer current, or otherwise protected against unintended use • If obsolete, are retained for legal or other purposes and properly identified Documents shall be legible, dated, kept orderly, readily identifiable, and retained for a specified period. [Implied documentation] Procedures and responsibilities to create and modify documentation.	

Table 7.1. *Continued.*

Number	Section and Clause	Documentation Requirement or Implication	Records Requirement
4.4.6	**Operational control**	Documented procedures for situations where absence could lead to deviations from environmental policy, objectives, and targets; stipulated operating criteria. [Implied documentation] Procedures related to significant environmental aspects of goods and services used by the organization, and procedures and requirements communicated to suppliers.	
4.4.7	**Emergency preparedness and response**	[Implied documentation] Procedures to identify potential emergencies, and the organization's planned preparation and response to accidents and emergency situations, and for preventing and mitigating associated environmental impacts.	
4.5	**CHECKING AND CORRECTIVE ACTION**		
4.5.1	**Monitoring and measurement**	Documented procedures to regularly monitor and measure key characteristics of operations and activities posing potential significant impact to the environment. Documented procedure to periodically evaluate compliance with relevant environmental legislation and regulations.	Records of performance, relevant operational controls, and conformance to organization's environmental objectives and targets. Calibration and maintenance records of monitoring equipment retained according to organization's procedures.

Table 7.1. *Continued.*

Number	Section and Clause	Documentation Requirement or Implication	Records Requirement
4.5.2	**Nonconformance and corrective and preventive action**	[Implied documentation] Procedures to define responsibility and authority for handling and investigating nonconformance, acting to mitigate impacts, and to initiate and complete corrective and preventive action. Record in documented procedures any changes implemented as a result of corrective or preventive action.	
4.5.3	**Records**	[Implied documentation] Procedures to identify, maintain, and dispose of environmental records, including training records and results of audits and reviews. Documented retention times for records.	Records shall be legible, identifiable, and traceable to involved activity, product, or service; stored and maintained so they are readily retrievable and protected against damage, deterioration, and loss. Maintain records to demonstrate conformance to requirements of the standard.
4.5.4	**Environmental management system audit**	[Implied documentation] Procedures for periodic environmental management system audits. Procedures shall address scope of the audit, frequency and methodologies, responsibilities and requirements for conducting the audit, and methods for reporting results.	
4.6	**MANAGEMENT REVIEW**		Documented management reviews of the environmental management system to ensure its continuing suitability, adequateness, and effectiveness, and to identify opportunities for continual improvement.

procedures, employee handbooks, user manuals, and safety program documentation. A source of need in this case is *interested parties*, defined in the standard (Definition 3.11) as "individual or group concerned with or affected by the environmental performance of an organization" (see clause 4.3.3, Objectives and targets). This could include employees, the general public, regulatory agencies, and many other parties. Another source of need that must be satisfied are legal requirements (see clause 4.3.2, Legal and other requirements). The litmus test of Nimble Documentation,® along with the focus on sources of need, is implied by clause 4.3.3.

> *When establishing and reviewing its objectives, an organization shall consider the legal and other requirements, its significant environmental aspects, its technological options and its financial, operational and business requirements, and the views of interested parties. (ASQC, ISO, and ANSI 1996, 3)*

An important feature of Nimble Documentation® applies to ISO 14001. The standard was designed to allow for a wide range of documentation associated with an environmental management system, but also to minimize the documentation burden placed on compliant organizations. In fact, the standard itself nearly paraphrases a central tenet of zero-based documentation: Documented procedures are required only "where their absence could lead to deviations from the environmental policy and the objectives and targets" (ASQC, ISO, and ANSI 1996, 4).

A world-class organization's financial, operational, and business requirements would not be met by environmental management documentation that was unnecessary or by the omission of documentation that *was*. And it behooves such an organization to continue to improve existing environmental management documentation, for example, to lower costs, facilitate access, and keep information up to date.

E. Additional Applications

Applying the zero-based approach and the litmus test to directive documentation and maintaining continuous measured process improvement can help an organization satisfy its sources of need, including legal and other requirements; improve quality; and save time and resources. In this chapter, Nimble Documentation® processes were shown to apply to employee handbooks, user manuals, safety programs, and ISO 14001. In the next chapter, the approach will be shown to apply equally as well to documentation relatives, such as records, forms, and approval authority systems. What other documentation would benefit from becoming more nimble?

Documentation required to comply with other standards is an obvious candidate.

QS-9000, the quality requirement unveiled by the big three auto makers (Chrysler, Ford, and General Motors) in 1994, expands ISO 9001 requirements. It adds three sector-specific requirements: the production part approval process, continuous improvement, and manufacturing capabilities. QS-9000 also includes customer-specific requirements for each of the three auto makers. Documentation requirements of the standard are the same as ISO 9001's, plus warrants (an industry standard document), controlled drawings and design changes, preliminary process performance results for critical characteristics, appearance approval reports, inspection results, laboratory test reports, process flow diagrams, and many others. Some have estimated the QS-9000 documentation requirements at three times ISO 9001's. Should an organization become QS-9000 registered? Both General Motors and Chrysler mandated that its suppliers become registered to the standard by 1997. At press time, Ford is considering it.

Should a supplier adopt the Nimble Documentation® approach? Because the auto makers by definition are their suppliers' customers, or a source of need, it would make no sense for prudent suppliers to ignore the standard—a voice of the customer. Furthermore, no supplier can remain globally competitive buried in documentation that needlessly constrains processes, is costly to maintain, or exposes the supplier to liability. Likewise, no supplier should do without documentation whose absence would be harmful.

Other industries that require documentation to comply with regulations and specialized quality standards include health care, food, pharmaceuticals, energy, communications, government, education, and hospitality.

When you think of documentation that can help an organization become more competitive—trim, flexible, accessible, and responsive to change—think of overhead transparencies and presentation software. Think of proposals, training manuals, and reports and think of performance evaluations, memos, and letters. Then apply the methodology of Nimble Documentation.®

CHAPTER 8

Documentation Relatives

> Solutions presented in this chapter address documentation challenges such as
>
> - How to develop a records retention program that minimizes both liability and expense
> - The benefits of automated forms
> - How to minimize the time and expense of processing forms
> - How to streamline an approval authority system

A world-class documentation system integrates directive document relatives. Inconsistent, disorganized, or bloated records, forms, and approval authority systems can muddle or clog an otherwise nimble system of policies, procedures, and work instructions. On the other hand, by applying the zero-based approach (see Chapter 2), these related components can strengthen and simplify business processes and they can reduce or conserve operating expenses. Quality standards, such as the ISO 9000 series, require documented, managed records relating to the quality of an organization's products or services (see Chapter 6). An environmental management system standard, such as ISO 14001, specifies or implies records maintenance, retention, and disposition (see Chapter 7). Also, prudent business requires a controlled records retention system to contain the costly runaway records proliferation that often results from an organization's information explosion.

Well-structured and sensibly managed company forms can make it easier for internal and external customers to communicate with an organization and maneuver through administrative transactions quickly. Authorization for committing company funds or other resources is a legal requirement; adopting a system that communicates that authority readily and clearly is smart.

This chapter presents the foundation for a practical and legally accepted records retention program and describes a popular seven-step method for developing a program that shares features with the zero-based approach to documentation. The chapter also addresses efficient forms and elements of a trim, responsive approval authority system.

A. Records

"Our records have grown out of control. Each year we create or receive mounds of paper records, generate stacks of computer printouts and produce cabinets full of microfilm and other duplicate records. The next year the volume increases even more." In *Records Retention Procedures* (1994), Donald S. Skupsky presents a convincing case for companies to establish a consistent, organized, and economical records retention program. The information explosion has created a records explosion. Companies keep records indefinitely as protection against litigation, but ironically end up supporting their adversaries' cases with subpoenaed information that should have been destroyed long ago. To the legal argument for a strong records retention program, Skupsky adds the costs of space, staff, equipment, and supplies for unnecessary or risky records and the need to readily access valuable and current information. His case is compelling.

The ISO 9000 series of quality system standards is another good reason to establish a nimble, comprehensive records retention program. As shown in Table 6.1, ISO 9000 certification requires records maintenance in many areas, such as section 4.1.3, Management review of the quality system; 4.3.4, Contract review; and 4.6.2, Acceptable subcontractors. (For an in-depth analysis of ISO 9000 records requirements, see Eugenia K. Brumm's book *Managing Records for ISO 9000 Compliance*, 1995.) Referencing applicable records directly in quality system documents or linking to them on-line, such as in operating procedures, saves users' time.

Traditionally, a records retention program establishes retention schedules for each of up to thousands of individual entries. Usually, the program and retention schedule access are designed around precise record titles and the department responsible for each record. The problem is that, when companies reorganize or departments simply change names (a common occurrence in firms subscribing to continuous process improvement and in mergers and acquisitions), records are difficult to locate. Staff members are challenged by obsolete, inaccessible records and companies are faced with high maintenance costs.

Skupsky's solution is four integrated files or reports: (1) legal research index, (2) legal group file, (3) records retention schedule, and (4) records listing with retention periods. The beauty of Skupsky's method is that, by classifying information into logical units, it can be processed economically as grouped data rather than individual data points.

The legal research index is organized by legal group code and subject and by the laws regarding retention. Table 8.1 shows the jurisdiction, the location where the law applies (Jur.); citation, the 14-digit code used to identify laws, from *Legal Requirements for Business Records* (LRBR Code); subject of the law; legal group code; legal period of retention; and the records affected and agency responsible for administering the law. Second is the legal group file, which classifies and codes laws into related groups and assigns a retention period for each group. Table 8.2 shows the legal group, subject, description, legal requirements, legal considerations, and total retention period for legal purposes. Next, the records retention schedule places related records into coded categories, and includes descriptions, retention periods, retention periods for copies, and offices responsible for the categorized records (see Table 8.3). Last in Skupsky's retention method is a records listing, with retention periods, that flows down from the coded schedule (see Table 8.4). Figure 8.1 is a checklist to help developers determine the scope of legal research required for a records retention program (Skupsky 1994).

The seven-step method for developing a records retention program shares features with the zero-based approach to documentation. The method's nimbleness lies in its purposeful approach, that is, retaining records only if and as long as required by several sources of need, for example, customers—including executives, accounting, legal functions, and other administrative functions—and laws. Skupsky's method also reduces development and maintenance costs by grouping and coding records with similar requirements and by avoiding assigning individual records to departments. The seven steps follow, but readers should refer to *Records Retention Procedures* (Skupsky

Table 8.1. Sample legal research index.

Jur.	Citation	LRBR Code	Subjects	Legal Group	Legal Period	Records Affected/Agency
US	26 CFR 1.6001-1	US 226-0970-00	tax income	ACC000	IND	accounting records Internal Revenue Service
US	26 CFR 31.6001-1	US 226-1090-00	tax employment	ACC000	4	payroll records Internal Revenue Service
US	26 CFR 31.6001-2	US 226-1100-00	tax employment	ACC000	4	payroll records Internal Revenue Service
US	26 CFR 31.6001-4	US 226-1130-00	tax employment	ACC000	4	payroll records; unemployment taxes Internal Revenue Service
US	26 CFR 31.6001-5	US 226-1150-00	tax employment	ACC000	4	payroll records Internal Revenue Service
US	26 CFR 301.6501(A)-1	US 226-1870-00	tax income— assessment general	ACC000	AS3	accounting records Internal Revenue Service
US	26 CFR 301.6501(C)-1	US 226-1880-00	tax income— assessment fraud	ACC000	ASIN	accounting records Internal Revenue Service
US	26 CFR 301.6501(E)-1	US 226-1890-00	tax gift— assessment understatement by 25%	ACC000	AS6	accounting records Internal Revenue Service
US	26 CFR 301.6501(E)-1	US 226-1890-00	tax income— assessment understatement by 25%	ACC000	AS6	accounting records Internal Revenue Service
US	26 CFR 301.6532-1(A)	US 226-1960-00	tax income—suit	ACC000	LA2	accounting records Internal Revenue Service
US	26 CFR 301.6532-2	US 226-1970-00	tax income—suit	ACC000	LA2	accounting records Internal Revenue Service
US	29 CFR 5.5	US 229-0040-00	contract federal—payroll	ACC000	3	payroll records Labor, Department of
US	29 CFR 516.5	US 229-0300-00	employment payroll records	ACC000	3	payroll records Labor, Department of: Wage and Hour Division
US	29 CFR 1620.22(B)	US 229-0910-00	limitation of actions wages, recovery of	ACC000	LA3	payroll records Equal Employment Opportunity Commission

Source: Donald S. Skupsky, *Records Retention Procedures,* Englewood, Colo.: Information Requirements Clearinghouse, 1994. Used with permission.

Table 8.2. Sample legal group file.

Legal Group	Subject	Description				Legal Requirements	Legal Considerations	Total
ACC000	Accounting/Tax General	Includes tax assessment or specific tax requirements for accounts payable, accounts receivable, etc.						
		Legal Requirements:	Minimum	TX: TTC 111.0041		3		
			Maximum	US: 26 CFR 31.6001-1		4		
			Selected	US: 26 CFR 31.6001-1		4		
		Legal Considerations:	Minimum	US: 26 USC 6532			LA1	
			Maximum	US: 26 CFR 301.6501(C)-1			ASIND	
			Selected	US: 26 CFR 301.6501(E)-1			6	
		Selected Legal Retention Period						6
ACC100	Accounting/Tax Capital Acquisitions	Includes depreciation, capital gains and losses, and repairs for capital property						
		Legal Requirements:	Minimum	US: 26 CFR 1.167(E)-1		ACT		
			Maximum	US: 26 CFR 1.167(E)-1		ACT		
			Selected	US: 26 CFR 1.167(E)-1		ACT		
		Legal Considerations:	Minimum	US: 26 CFR 301.6501(A)-1			AS3	
			Maximum	US: 26 CFR 301.6501(C)-1			IND	
			Selected	US: 26 CFR 301.6501(A)-1			6	
		Selected Legal Retention Period						ACT+6
ADV000	Advertising Packaging/ Labeling	Includes laws related to promotions, introductory offers, product size advantages, etc.						
		See MAN100 for product liability considerations.						
		Legal Requirements:	Minimum	US: 16 CFR 502.101		1		
			Maximum	US: 16 CFR 502.101		1		
			Selected	US: 16 CFR 502.101		1		
		Legal Considerations:	Minimum	TX: 16.003			LA2	
			Maximum	TX: 16.003			LA2	
			Selected	TX: 16.003/LIABILITY CONCERNS			ACT+2	
		Selected Legal Retention Period						ACT+2

Source: Donald S. Skupsky, *Records Retention Procedures,* Englewood, Colo.: Information Requirements Clearinghouse, 1994. Used with permission.

Table 8.3. Sample records retention schedule.

Retention code	Retention Category Descriptive/Cross Reference	Legal Group	Retention of Official Records				Retention of Copies	Office of Record
			Legal	User	Other	Total		
ACC1000	**Accounting** **Accounts Payable/Receivable** Records related to payment of financial obligations and receipt of revenues. Includes vouchers, vendor invoices and statements; payroll and payroll deductions; government contracts and grants, contributions, and other income.	ACC000	6	3	0	6	MAX1	Accounting
ACC1010	**Accounting** **Journals/Ledgers** Records used to transfer charges between accounts and for summarizing account information. Final, annual records only.	ACC000	6	10	0	10	MAX1	Accounting
ACC2000	**Accounting** **Capital Property** Includes purchase and sales of property and equipment, depreciation, improvements, etc. Includes financial obligations associated with capital expenditures, purchase of land, buildings, equipment, furnishings, motor vehicles; material transfers, work orders, additions or improvements to building or equipment, property reporting.	ACC100	ACT+6	ACT	0	ACT+6	MAX5	Accounting
ACC9900	**Accounting** **General** Records related to accounting records not previously covered. Includes accounting reports, control documents; system input, maintenance and changes.	NONE	0	3	0	3	MAX1	Accounting

Source: Donald S. Skupsky, *Records Retention Procedures,* Englewood, Colo.: Information Requirements Clearinghouse, 1994. Used with permission.

Table 8.4. Sample records listing with retention periods.

Department/Location Record Series	Record Code	Retention Category	Legal Group	Retention of Official Records				Retention of Copies	Office of Record	Status
				Legal	User	Other	Total			
Accounting										
Accounts Payable										
accounts payable	ACC-00-01	ACC1000	ACC000	6	3	0	6	MAX1	Accounting	Official
accounts payable invoices	ACC-00-02	ACC1000	ACC000	6	3	0	6	MAX1	Accounting	Official
accounts payable ledgers	ACC-00-03	ACC1010	ACC000	6	10	0	10	MAX1	Accounting	Official
amortization records	ACC-00-04	ACC1000	ACC000	6	3	0	6	MAX1	Accounting	Official
bills	ACC-00-05	ACC1000	ACC000	6	3	0	6	MAX1	Accounting	Official
cash disbursements	ACC-00-06	ACC1000	ACC000	6	3	0	6	MAX1	Accounting	Official
commission statements	ACC-00-07	MIS1000	NONE	0	1	0	1	MAX1	Various	Official
cost accounting records	ACC-00-08	ACC1000	ACC000	6	3	0	6	MAX1	Accounting	Official
cost sheets	ACC-00-09	ACC1000	ACC000	6	3	0	6	MAX1	Accounting	Official
cost statements	ACC-00-10	ACC1000	ACC000	6	3	0	6	MAX1	Accounting	Official
credit card charge slips	ACC-00-11	ACC1000	ACC000	6	3	0	6	MAX1	Accounting	Official
credit card statements	ACC-00-12	ACC1000	ACC000	6	3	0	6	MAX1	Accounting	Official
debit advices	ACC-00-13	ACC1000	ACC000	6	3	0	6	MAX1	Accounting	Official
donations	ACC-00-14	ACC1000	ACC000	6	3	0	6	MAX1	Accounting	Official
expense reports	ACC-00-15	ACC1000	ACC000	6	3	0	6	MAX1	Accounting	Official
invoices	ACC-00-16	ACC1000	ACC000	6	3	0	6	MAX1	Accounting	Official
petty cash records	ACC-00-17	ACC1000	ACC000	6	3	0	6	MAX1	Accounting	Official
property taxes	ACC-00-18	ACC1000	ACC000	6	3	0	6	MAX1	Accounting	Official
purchase requisitions	ACC-00-19	FIN8000	NONE	0	3	0	3	MAXI	Finance	Official
royalty payments	ACC-00-20	ACC1000	ACC000	6	3	0	6	MAXI	Accounting	Official
travel expenses	ACC-00-21	ACC1000	ACC000	6	3	0	6	MAXI	Accounting	Official
unemployment insurance payments	ACC-00-22	ACC1000	ACC000	6	3	0	6	MAXI	Accounting	Official
vouchers	ACC-00-23	ACC1000	ACC000	6	3	0	6	MAX1	Accounting	Official
workers compensation insurance payments	ACC-00-24	ACC1000	ACC000	6	3	0	6	MAX1	Accounting	Official
Accounts Receivable										
accounts receivable	ACC-10-01	ACC1000	ACC000	6	3	0	6	MAX1	Accounting	Official
accounts receivable ledgers	ACC-10-02	ACC1010	ACC000	6	10	0	10	MAX1	Accounting	Official
cash books	ACC-10-03	ACC1010	ACC000	6	10	0	10	MAX1	Accounting	Official

Source: Donald S. Skupsky, *Records Retention Procedures*, Englewood, Colo.: Information Requirements Clearinghouse, 1994. Used with permission.

1. **General Business Activities**
   - ☐ Business Organization
     - ☐ Corporation
     - ☐ Corporation, Professional
     - ☐ Partnership
     - ☐ Partnership, Limited
     - ☐ Sole Proprietorship
   - ☐ Employment/Personnel
   - ☐ Tax/Accounting
   - ☐ _____

2. **Record Locations**
   - ☐ Country
     - ☐ United States
     - ☐ Canada
     - ☐ _____
   - ☐ States/Provinces
     - ☐ _____
     - ☐ _____
     - ☐ _____
     - ☐ _____
   - ☐ Local Government
     - ☐ _____
     - ☐ _____

3. **Regulatory Agencies**
   - ☐ Federal
     - ☐ Agriculture
     - ☐ Defense
     - ☐ Energy
       - ☐ Federal Energy Regulatory
     - ☐ Environmental Protection Agency
     - ☐ Federal Deposit and Insurance Corp.
     - ☐ Health and Human Services
     - ☐ Housing and Urban Development
     - ☐ Labor
       - ☐ Employment and Training
       - ☐ Employment Standards
       - ☐ Equal Employment Opportunity
       - ☐ Occupational Safety and Health
       - ☐ Wage and Hour
       - ☐ _____
     - ☐ Securities and Exchange Commission

3. **Regulatory Agencies (cont.)**
   - ☐ Federal (cont.)
     - ☐ Small Business Administration
     - ☐ Transportation
     - ☐ Treasury
       - ☐ Alcohol, Tobacco and Firearms
       - ☐ Internal Revenue Service
     - ☐ _____
     - ☐ _____
   - ☐ State/Local
     - ☐ Labor
     - ☐ Revenue
     - ☐ _____
     - ☐ _____
     - ☐ _____
     - ☐ _____

4. **Industry**
   - ☐ Agriculture
   - ☐ Banking
   - ☐ Communications
   - ☐ Construction
   - ☐ Education
   - ☐ Health Care
   - ☐ Manufacturing
   - ☐ Petroleum
   - ☐ Transportation
   - ☐ Utility
   - ☐ _____
   - ☐ _____

5. **Products/Activities**
   - ☐ _____
   - ☐ _____
   - ☐ _____

6. **Other Regulated Areas**
   - ☐ Advertising
   - ☐ Consumer Protection
   - ☐ Environment
     - ☐ Air Pollution
     - ☐ Land/Water Pollution
     - ☐ _____
   - ☐ _____
   - ☐ _____

Source: Donald S. Skupsky, *Records Retention Procedures*, Englewood, Colo.: Information Requirements Clearinghouse, 1994. Used with permission.

Figure 8.1. Determining the scope of legal research.

1994) for details on developing a nimble, comprehensive records retention program.

1. *Complete preliminary procedures.* Obtain approval and support for the program; inventory existing records maintained by the organization; and determine organizational structure activities, business locations, and regulatory agencies.

2. *Research laws.* Review applicable laws; include legal counsel.

3. *Extract key legal information.* Use relevant laws from the Legal Research Index, which is easier to review than the laws' full text.

4. *Assign applicable laws to groups and determine legal retention periods.* Assigning to legal groups the hundreds of laws that typically affect an organization's records retention eliminates the need to refer to each law individually.

5. *Develop the retention schedule.* Identify the functional retention categories that correspond to the records inventory. Fewer than 100 categories usually will suffice. Define the types of records covered by each category. Determine initial user retention periods and any other retention periods. Assign legal groups to the functional retention categories. Indicate the total retention category, which is the longest of the legal, user, or other retention periods. Determine the office responsible for maintaining official records for the total retention period. Other groups will maintain records according to the period indicated for copies.

> **Checklist 8.1:**
> **Steps for Developing a Zero-Based Records Retention Program** (drawn from Skupsky 1994)
>
> ☐ Complete preliminary procedures.
> ☐ Research laws.
> ☐ Extract key legal information.
> ☐ Assign laws to groups; determine legal retention periods.
> ☐ Develop retention schedule.
> ☐ Assign functional retention category to each record.
> ☐ Revise the four integrated retention files and reports.

6. *Assign a functional retention category to each record listed in the inventory.* The records retention period for the category becomes the period for the record series. Generate a report with records retention periods.

7. *Revise the four integrated retention files and reports (legal research index, legal group file, records retention schedule, and records listing with retention periods).* Develop procedures on records destruction, documentation, program revision, training, and any other implementation issues. Distribute the draft schedules and procedures for review. Prepare the records retention program manual and obtain approval.

Following Skupsky's seven-step method fits a handle around records retention requirements, but it does not address the other essential elements of archiving documentation: prevention, preparation, and recovery of damaged or lost documentation, and the more mundane issue of document history files.

It takes only one experience crashing a hard disk with critical or hard to reconstruct information for most people to start backing up document files routinely. Unfortunately, many people's idea of data protection is to copy files to a floppy disk and keep it in a cabinet or drawer. Some keep the backups right next to the computer. It is not difficult to imagine that some disasters will affect all property at the same location. Maybe a crashed hard disk won't damage a floppy disk, but a fire can burn the computer *and* the backup near it. Earthquakes in California, Mexico, and Japan; hurricanes in North Carolina; floods in Missouri; power surges in France—no site is safe from natural or human-caused disasters. A sensible program will protect important information and assist in recovery in case damage or loss cannot be prevented.

For office backups, devices such as tape systems and zip drives offer convenient document backup storage. A Bernoulli drive is another, removable alternative. Each of these systems works better than an assortment of floppy disks and each is faster and easier to transport. But documentation functions also need to establish remote storage capabilities in the event of wider ranging disasters.

A reciprocal arrangement works well for some departments, whereby a function mails documentation copies regularly, say, weekly, to an offsite location more than a couple of hundred miles away. The recipient function does the same. Each time a new backup arrives, the old one is rotated out. Some companies transfer backed up files electronically. With the reciprocal system, the potential for lost documentation is no greater than one week's worth. Every company documentation function should have a written procedure for recovering information in an emergency (the procedure should be stored at more than one site, of course). Sound on-line document storage and retrieval systems include regular backups and remote rotating storage.

Another important consideration for records is audit trails. Hansel's trail of crumbs became a lifeline for the storybook character and his sister. Indexed history files serve the same purpose for organizations. Auditors or legal specialists research files to determine the company policies and practices that were in effect at a given time. Records may be subpoenaed by former employees who claim the company acted wrongfully. Suppliers request reviews of purchase orders. Often, the outcomes of litigation depend on the integrity of the history files. The economy of locating obsolete documents quickly contributes to an organization's financial good health. A history or audit trail becomes especially important when major reorganizations or document streamlining efforts rearrange or delete documents or parts of them.

To preserve a clear audit trail, maintain a matrix of documents and their revisions by number and topic and information deleted from them. Notate an organization chart matrix with old and new names for an organization or their parts. Maintain a master (and a backup of the master) of each document revision. To avoid obsolete copies being mistaken for current versions, stamp every obsolete hard copy master with words such as *History files* or *Reference only.* Protect electronic history masters from revision.

B. Forms

Think of a form as an information template, an efficient vehicle for gathering the same kind of information from many sources. A nimble form does not surprise its users. It does not cause confusion or waste its users' time. A nimble form is clear. The best are self-explanatory. The next best include instructions on the reverse side, if hard copy, or on the front, if generated by computer. Instructions on the form avoid detours to a procedures manual.

To facilitate information entry, processing, and retrieval, maintain the expected order of fields or elements. For example, if an organization's standard memorandum lists *Date* first, then *To,* next *From,* and finally *Subject,* maintain that order for all memos. Employees expecting to see the date first will be able to quickly file and retrieve documents chronologically. If they expect to see the subject last, they can thumb through a pile of memos briskly, scanning for a topic. If a group of forms requires the last name first, but a single form asks for the first name first, many people will complete the form incorrectly or cross out, white out, or erase information. Or they may rip up the form and start again. In any case, extra resources will be spent when they don't have to be.

Forms are standardized to facilitate compiling information. Sure, a user can write a freehand letter to carry the same information as a form; however, a bit of information omitted that a recipient requires will generate additional processing time. For example, a letter might not include a needed social security number. Then the recipient has to correspond, requesting more information, and the user has to correspond again. Placing a social security number field on a standardized form decreases the correspondence. Placing the field in an expected location on the form and clearly asking for the information further minimizes processing time.

Completed forms also serve as records and allow future users to locate information in history files faster.

Today, competitive organizations use forms that are automated at least to some extent. At the most basic level, form masters are created through word processing or other computer software or are purchased, copies are printed, and users complete the forms by typewriter or by hand. At the next level of automation, a copy is generated—printed—on demand and completed by typewriter or hand. Automation at the third level means a form is generated by computer and completed by computer. Standard word processing packages include this template function. Transactions conducted through forms can be approved by hand signature. Forms automated at the fourth level may be password approved. Also, information can be linked electronically to other automated forms and systems, for example, creating a paperless system that can eliminate opportunities for error by eliminating data reentry. Some systems use voice data entry and voice recognition for approval.

A forms improvement team at Hughes Ground Systems Group initiated an electronic forms library to be hosted on a LAN server. Before the improvement, individuals were recreating company forms on their computers throughout the Group. To assist its customers, the forms function planned to capture already created forms and add them to the on-line forms library. The team sent out notices to each division asking employees to share copies of their forms. The team reviewed the forms it received and selected and enhanced employees' versions to add to the library. After the forms were organized and indexed on a server, the team publicized their availability and instructions to access them.

Many organizations have a problem with too many forms. Or, there are too many form errors or omissions. The zero-based documentation approach works well for streamlining forms. First, apply the litmus test (questions one to four, following). Then ask about a nimbler way (question five).

1. Is the form required by law?

2. Is it specified by contract?

3. Is the form needed according to prudent business practices?

4. Will any harm come to the organization if the form is eliminated?

5. Does the form require expending the least amount of resources?

If the answer to each of the first four questions is "no," cancel the form. If at least one question warrants a "yes," and the answer to question five is "no" or "maybe," consider revising the form.

Following are a few ways to minimize the time and dollars spent on processing a form.

• *Name the form so its purpose is clear.* "Administrative Request" is too vague. Be more specific.

• *Maintain the expected order of fields.* Use organization-standard headers. Sequence fields logically, for example: chronological, most important information to least, or highest value item field to least value.

• *Avoid hiding small but essential fields where they may be overlooked.* A social security number field between two large comment boxes is easy to miss. Emphasize the field, for example, by surrounding it with space, using bolder text, or repositioning it to a more prominent location on the form.

• *Design the form to be clear without instructions.* However, if instructions *are* required, print them on the form itself, not in a procedure manual. Help users find information quickly.

• *Position field names clearly with their corresponding fields.* Don't make users guess whether they need to write above a field name or below it (or to the left or to the right of it).

• *Use a single form for multiple duty.* An HR department of a large company required four separate forms to process an employee transfer request: one for payroll, one for employee relations, one for the equal opportunity office, and one for the career development office. Much of the same information was required for each form. A single form could have been used to feed information into a database accessible by each of the four functions.

Checklist 8.2: Considerations for Nimble Forms

☐ Ensure the name shows form's purpose.

☐ Maintain expected order of fields.

☐ Don't hide small but critical fields.

☐ Make the form clear without instructions.

☐ If instructions are needed, print them on the form, not in a separate procedure.

☐ Position field names clearly with their corresponding fields.

☐ Use a single form for multiple duty.

☐ Identify each form with a number and revision date, keyed to other documentation.

☐ Avoid referencing names and telephone numbers.

• *Identify each form with a number and revision date.* Key the form number to other documentation covering the same function or process, such as an ISO 9001 quality system manual, standard operating procedures, or records (or all of these).

• *Avoid referencing individuals' names or telephone numbers, except if the form is on-line or otherwise economical to revise, or if the information is hard to find elsewhere.* Organizations change. Rerouting forms to other individuals or placing multiple telephone calls is expensive and delays transactions.

C. Approval Authority

Big, long-established companies tend to accumulate administrative processes that have outgrown their usefulness. After a while, nobody remembers why a process is required. For example, no one can figure out why six signature lines foot a standard company form, when only the last signatory seriously reviews the transaction authorized by the form. Everyone else assumes the person who signs just below *their* signature will do it. When questioned about signature line strata, people say, "That's the way we've always done it." Some small or new companies, not knowing a better way, emulate the established giants. Or, sometimes, upstarts have no consistent administrative processes in place, which is equally harmful. By trying to avoid anything that sounds bureaucratic, some firms—usually the ones most proud of their entrepreneurial culture—miss out on the benefits of standardized management and operating systems. For many organizations, approval authority is an archaic administrative process and often a terrific candidate for streamlining.

A cross-functional team at Hughes Ground Systems Group tested its belief that the multiple layers of signatures specified by forms for business transactions were rubber stamps and added little value to the authorization process. The team designed pilot projects in two functions to streamline transactions authorized by signed forms: finance and HR. The team interviewed transaction owners, those responsible for activity as a result of receiving a fully signed form. The results indicated that greater than 75 percent of the forms studied could be eliminated and, on the remaining ones, authorization signatures could be deleted completely or reduced significantly with no breach in legal, contractual, or prudent business requirements and no harm to the company (the litmus test for approval authority systems). Executive management supported pushing down administrative decisions closer to the operational level and eliminating unneeded higher layers of authorization. What manager wouldn't be grateful for a smaller pile of forms to sign?

The complexity of an approval authority system depends largely on the scope and complexity of an organization's products and services and the standards and regulations of its industry. But it also depends on the organization's leadership style or management culture. Whatever the complexity, however, the system should be communicated clearly to all participants and accessible by all who need to use it.

Many companies have placed their approval authority system on-line. Organizations link their directive documents and forms via an intranet. That way, with a click on a link an employee can find out who is authorized to approve a transaction specified in an operating procedure and he or she can authorize the transaction via an electronic form using a password instead of a written signature.

For more traditional, hard copy systems, a chart of approvals should be included in standard operating procedures or a policies handbook. Figure 8.2 shows a simple chart prepared for a small, young but rapidly growing service business. It communicates authority to approve transactions yet avoids administrative wastefulness and congestion. Note that formats for approving transactions are not limited to forms (Figure 8.2, paragraph 2.3).

Another chart of approvals (Figure 8.3), from an educational agency's policies and procedures handbook, identifies the executive and senior management positions by level and indicates the levels authorized to approve transactions listed by function or process. This chart was particularly important to the agency because it communicated information about forms consolidated from the merger of two organizations.

A discussion of approval authority systems would be incomplete without mentioning completely automated forms transmission. Generating forms electronically and then printing them out for a signature wastes valuable resources. One way to automate forms is to use encryption keys, which must be delivered or picked up (private key management) or distributed electronically, for example by e-mail (public key management). In simple terms, digital signatures are encrypted and decrypted, and both the message and the originator are authenticated.

**Checklist 8.3:
Considerations for
Charts of Approvals**

☐ Accessibility

☐ Date

☐ Scope

☐ Clarity

☐ Conditions for designees

☐ Conditions for alternates

☐ Method for indicating approval

☐ Acceptable formats (such as forms, POs)

☐ Authority for chart's contents

[Logo] XYZ Corporation		Operating Procedure
	Chart of Approvals	
		Number: XYZP 1-2-1
		Date: 8/7/96
		Page: 1 of 2

1.0 SCOPE

Applies to all employees at all XYZ Corporation facilities.

2.0 PROCEDURE

2.1 The personnel or functions designated in the chart below, or their designees, are authorized to approve specified transactions or commit company funds according to indicated conditions. Designees are authorized in writing.

2.2 Alternates are authorized to approve specified transactions or commit company funds only in the absence of the designated personnel or functions. Alternates may not authorize designees.

2.3 Written signatures or electronic passwords indicate approval. Formats for approval include, but are not limited to: forms, letters, memoranda, contracts, and purchase orders.

Transaction	Approval Authority	Alternate	Comments/Conditions
Compensation Increases	Compensation Committee		After Dept. Mgr. recommends
Contracts	President	Exec. VP	
Copy-[Confidential] Reports	Dept. Mgr.		After Copy Committee recommends
Corrective/Preventive Action	Dept. Mgr.		
Employee Discipline	Dept. Mgr.		
Employee Suggestions	Dept. Mgr.		
Expense Reimbursement	(See comments)		Required, in sequence: 1. Staff; 2. Dept. Mgr.; & 3. President or Finance Exec.
Facilities Upgrades/ Construction	President	Exec. VP	After Facilities Mgr. recommends
Hiring	Dept. Mgr.	HR Mgr.	

Figure 8.2. Example A of a chart of approvals.

[Logo] XYZ Corporation   **Operating Procedure**

Chart of Approvals

Number:	XYZP 1-2-1
Date:	8/7/96
Page:	2 of 2

Transaction	Approval Authority	Alternate	Comments/Conditions
Leaves	Dept. Mgr.	HR Mgr.	
Performance Appraisal	Dept. Mgr. & Compensation Committee		Both required
Project Authorization Request (PAR)	President	Exec. VP	After Dept. Mgr. approves
Promotion	Compensation Committee		After Dept. Mgr. recommends
Property Purchasing-Capital Purchasing-Office Supplies	Exec. VP Dept. Mgr.		
Receiving	Reception		
Safety	HR Mgr.		
Security-Locks	Facilities Mgr.		
Shipping	Admin. Asst.		
Telephones, 800 numbers	Facilities Mgr.		
Termination	Dept. Mgr.	HR Mgr.	
Training	Dept. Mgr.		
Transfer-Interdepartment	Transferring & Receiving Dept. Mgrs.		Both required
Travel	Dept. Mgr.		
Vacation	Dept. Mgr.		

I. A. Prove, Vice President, Administration

Figure 8.2. *Continued.*

Chart of Approvals

The following table indicates the authority to approve requests or specific documents committing Agency resources.

Key:

A - Chief Executive Officer
B - Chief Financial Officer
C - Deputy Director
D - Director, Administration and Finance
E - Contracts and Administrative Services Manager/Controller
F - Program Manager
G - Project Director

An X indicates authority to approve requests or commit Agency resources. No employee may approve his/her own request.

	Form	**A**	**B**	**C**	**D**	**E**	**F**	**G**	**Comments**
Business Operations									
Timesheets		X	X	X	X	X	X	X	
Local/Non-Local Expense Reports		X	X	X	X	X	X	X	
Mileage Reports		X	X	X	X	X	X	X	
Purchase Requests		X	X	X	X	X	X	X	
Purchase Orders		X	X		X				
Travel Authorizations		X	X	X	X	X	X	X	
Statements of Work Completed (Consultant)		X	X	X	X	X	X	X	
Requests for Space/Relocation		X	X	X	X				
Check Requests (only by prior authorization)		X	X	X	X	X			
Office Assignments		X	X						
Contracts for Services (Consultant)		X	X		X				
Relocation Expenses		X	X	X	X				¹
Personnel Operations									
Leaves of Absence		X	X		X				¹

Authority Levels

Figure 8.3. Example B of a chart of approvals.

Form	A	B	C	D	E	F	G	Comments
Notices of Appointment (Exempt)			X					[1]
Notices of Appointment (Non-Exempt)			X					[1]
Requests for Regular Employee	X	X	X	X				[1]
Requests for Temporary Employee	X	X	X	X	X	X	X	[2]
Timesheet Revisions	X	X	X	X				
Personnel Action Notices	X	X	X	X				[1]
Overtime Authorizations	X	X	X	X	X	X	X	
Proposals, Grants, and Contracts	(Refer to Proposal Development Procedures.)							
Intent to Propose (ITP)	X		X					
Proposals	X		X					
Contracts and Grants[3]	X	X		X				
Teaming Agreements	X	X		X				
Equity Expenditure Request	X	X		X				
Subcontracts	X	X						
Financial								
Investments	X	X		X				
Leases and Rental Transactions	X	X		X				
Attorney Fees	X	X	X	X				
Bad Debt Settlements and Charge-off of Delinquent Accounts	X	X	X	X				
Disposal of Agency-Owned Assets	X	X	X	X				

1. Signature approval of the Deputy Director of Human Resources is required in addition to any other indicated level.

2. Signature approval of Controller is required in addition to any other indicated level.

3. Only officers of the Agency are authorized to sign any document that legally binds the Agency. This includes contracts, memoranda of understanding, letters of agreement, maintenance agreements, purchase orders, etc.

Figure 8.3. *Continued.*

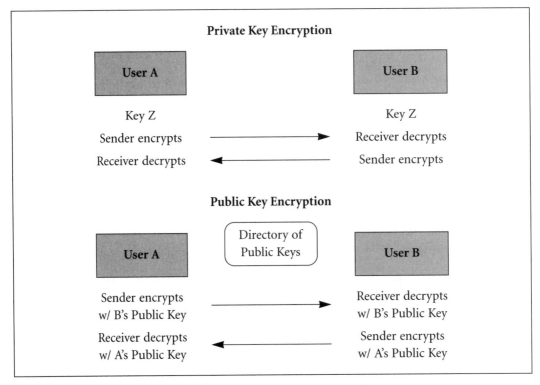

Source: Kibbee Streetman, "Who Holds the Keys to Encrypted Electronic Documents?" *Technologies for Managing Information,* ARMA International, Vol. 1, No. 4, May 1996. Used with permission.

Figure 8.4. Private key encryption and public key encryption.

Figure 8.4 diagrams how the keys work. Standards for encryption keys already exist and wide applications are being developed. The U.S. Postal Service will act as a repository for public key certificates containing information identifying each user. Others can then retrieve certificates from the service to authenticate digital signatures. Automated forms are becoming common in progressive organizations.

CHAPTER 9

Documentation Center of Excellence

Solutions presented in this chapter address documentation challenges such as

- What are the basic characteristics of a documentation COE?
- What are the benefits and drawbacks of outsourcing and insourcing documentation services?
- What skills are needed by empowered documentation staff?
- How do you develop effective self-directed documentation teams?
- What characterizes the most effective focus groups for writing procedures?
- What is the role of training in a documentation COE?
- What factors contribute to accountability?
- What is the relationship between a documentation COE and team performance evaluation?

A COE is a way to bring together a company's capabilities to produce a peerless, specialized product or process. COEs exploit the synergy of top talent working together and the economies of standardized facilities and equipment. Design COEs traditionally cluster engineering expertise to focus on a single product or family of products or processes. Production COEs typically consolidate state-of-the-art manufacturing capabilities. Administrative COEs, such as purchasing functions, take advantage of volume processing and streamlined resources. A documentation COE is no different. It draws together expertise, facilities, and equipment to deliver Nimble Documentation®, for example, trained teams, hub-arranged offices, and standardized software.

This chapter, the last in the *Application* topic group, defines a documentation COE and presents options for organizations that wish to establish, improve, or contract for documentation services. First, COE characteristics are described, then the advantages and disadvantages of outsourcing and insourcing the function are illustrated. Next is a discussion of the skills required for COE personnel and then exploration of self-directed documentation teams. The chapter also identifies personnel roles and responsibilities, and training. Finally, it addresses accountability for the function and performance evaluation.

A. Characteristics of a Documentation COE

Whether deployed by an internal S&P organization, a documentation consultant or outsourcing firm, or document "owner" (function responsible for content), a documentation COE displays four basic characteristics. It is

- Responsive to customers and other sources of need
- Streamlined
- Empowered
- Quality managed

Consider each of the four COE characteristics followed by examples of how organizations have demonstrated those characteristics.

Responsive to customers and other sources of need. Responsive documentation requires continuously assessing customers' needs (such as readers, users, and subject matter owners) and legal and other requirements. Assessments include questionnaires and surveys, hotline call analyses, web site hits, and piloted instructions. Analytical reports that show quickly and clearly the benefit to the reader or to the goals of the reader's organization are responsive documentation. Responsiveness is easier user access to information, lower cost of an on-line versus hard copy documentation system, or improved technical service speed and accuracy. Regularly reviewing legal and other requirements and maintaining regular contact with representatives of standards and audit organizations also help to ensure responsiveness to need.

• *Assess customer requirements.* S&P analysts asked users if they wanted to be included in e-mail notification of new, revised, or canceled company bulletins. They sent messages to users whose names were on hard copy distribution lists.

• *Provide access.* A process improvement team gave presentations and held question and answer sessions at division staff meetings to learn how operating procedures could be made more accessible. A county probation department trained its managers and supervisors to write court reports with facts and numerical data presented early in the reports to help judges quickly reach the most important information.

• *Simplify.* A quality engineer and S&P manager co-facilitated a focus group of document owners to eliminate redundant sections of the company's quality system practices.

• *Contain or reduce costs.* A cross-functional team reengineered a forms system and drastically cut warehouse floor space and leasing costs.

• *Respond with speed and accuracy.* An organization chart function with vocal support of executive management shaved days off the average turnaround time for preparing and distributing charts.

The County of Los Angeles contracted to train its managers and supervisors to write analytically. One of the goals was to achieve a customer or "you" attitude in memos, court reports, performance evaluations, and other strategic documents. In this public system, heavy workloads and limited resources mean every piece of writing must connect quickly with a customer's needs. Showing the benefit to the reader, the "you" attitude saves the reader time, and often rescues a document from needless return cycles, or worse, the bottom of a pile (see Chapter 5).

Checklist 9.1: Characteristics of a Documentation COE

☐ Responsive to customers and other sources of need
  ☐ Assess customer requirements
  ☐ Provide access
  ☐ Simplify
  ☐ Contain or reduce costs
  ☐ Respond with speed and accuracy
☐ Streamlined
☐ Empowered
  ☐ Skilled to do the job
  ☐ Committed to satisfy customers
  ☐ Strong positive attitude
  ☐ Willing to accept accountability for actions
  ☐ Able to communicate effectively
  ☐ Invested in resources for improvement
☐ Quality managed

Streamlined. Nimble organizations streamline their processes by eliminating non–value-added activities and unneeded documentation (see Chapter 2) and by standardization (see Chapter 4). Manufacturing organizations historically have streamlined their processes through a variety of initiatives, including time and motion studies, quality circles and other tools for improvement, and standardized production. Organizations have begun to turn their attention to administrative functions, such as documentation, as prime candidates for streamlining. Following are a few documentation streamlining initiatives implemented at Hughes. Employees

• Reduced volume, simplified language, and consolidated written practices of four former Groups in conjunction with the company's strategic initiative to streamline all directive documents.

• Established and used lesson plans for both IBM and Macintosh access developed by the S&P function for the Videotex system. At the time, the function had just adopted a mainframe-based information storage and retrieval system customized from Videotex software. Because S&P personnel specified the system and knew its capabilities, and could relate to users in lay terms, they developed plans to train users on the system.

• Reduced the volume of organization charts and their processing cycle time. The company structure was changing rapidly. Charts for lower level organizations, especially, were almost always obsolete, often before they were published. The function responsible for organization charts imported a facilitator from the quality division to help a team streamline chart processing and drive responsibility for lower-level charts down to the organizations. The results were a 46 percent decrease in volume and an approximately equal reduction in average cycle time to publish a chart from draft to distribution.

• Increased inventory turns for forms. The forms inventory system was revamped by a cross-functional team comprised of forms administration, purchasing, and graphic arts staff. The team reduced warehouse floor space from 3250 to 479 square feet, a savings of approximately 85 percent. Outsourcing the system to a forms management company provided additional benefits.

Empowered. Technology has been fairly impressive for managing documentation, but no factor is more critical to Nimble Documentation® than empowered personnel.

World-class organizations recognize that company chiefs can know less than 5 percent of each company operation. A well-trained workforce that has clearly defined roles and responsibilities takes initiative toward meeting organizational goals, is held accountable for performance, and is the difference between an organization that competes successfully and one that watches on the sidelines.

Much like *reengineering,* the term *empowerment* has been misunderstood, overused, and misapplied. To many, it means unled and unmanaged employees, permissiveness, carte blanche, and anything goes. This is not empowerment for world-class documentation.

One definition of empowerment is "having the authority and responsibility to make the decisions and take the actions necessary to improve your work" (The Forum Corporation 1992). To be empowered, individuals must have

- The skills to do their job
- The commitment to satisfy their customers
- A strong positive attitude
- The willingness to accept accountability for their actions
- The ability to communicate effectively
- Investment resources for improvement, including people, dollars, information, and equipment

Documentation nimbleness requires an empowered workforce, which includes skilled personnel, self-direction, clear roles and responsibilities, cutting-edge training, accountable performance, constructive performance evaluation, and adequate resources. The following exemplify employee empowerment.

• A documentation COE achieved 100 percent participation in continuous measurable improvement teams. Every function, every task, and every staff member was expected to lead or contribute in other ways to at least one process improvement team. It was not enough for employees to do a satisfactory job of performing to the department's SORs. The COE demanded teams to benchmark and exceed the best by reducing processing time for organization charts, implementing error-free practices, developing e-mail distribution of bulletins, and creating password approved on-line forms. Self-directed teams evolved from these focused work team accomplishments.

• One hundred percent of staff trained in continuous measurable improvement processes. An empowered staff is a knowledgeable, skilled staff. Every member of the COE participated in training that included quality tools, metrics, team dynamics, process mapping, and other critical elements. Some members also were trained in team leadership.

• A self-directed team of documentation analysts reached consensus on objectives that flowed down from company goals. The team members refined the company's team performance appraisal and planning process and form and administered it to support performance that met or exceeded objectives and planned course corrections for performance that did not. Team members participated in work assignment decisions. A team empowered meant a team accountable.

Quality managed. The TQM philosophy begins with leadership commitment to initiate and sustain managed improvement. It embraces all of a company's operations and all of its employees. It is not a program *du jour,* a quick fix that an executive introduces (and forgets) after reading about it in an in-flight magazine. A documentation COE breathes TQM; every aspect of the organization is devoted to quality from continuously assessing the needs of software user manual readers to rearranging a group's offices to facilitate team consulting. The following few examples characterize a quality managed documentation function.

• A team installed monitors in a cafeteria so computerless colleagues could access on-line bulletins.

• Monthly metrics indicated that a function responsible for writing and editing company documentation maintained publication of error-free practices and procedures so consistently that it was awarded world-class status for zero defects.

B. Outsourcing and Insourcing

Why would an organization want to outsource a documentation function? This section addresses the benefits and the drawbacks of outsourcing—and briefly discusses insourcing—and lists considerations for seeking outside documentation assistance.

Outsourcing has become a global megatrend for business. Employee leasing, accounting services, back office management, and many other outsourced functions help companies not only cut operating costs but also reshape the way they do business. Organizations have benefited from the specialization, skills, and quality of outsourced functions. Outsourcing lets companies focus their resources on core business.

Insourcing is a newer term. To some, it means that a contracting firm or consultant manages internal staff, in other words, outsourcing inside.

Employees continue to work for a company, but an outsider manages the function. Others interpret insourcing as transferring responsibilities for a function to specialists inside a company. For example, rather than having a quality assurance employee write a quality manual, and an employee from data processing document computing procedures, and then someone from accounting write a cashier's desk instructions, a documentation function assumes responsibility for all three activities. Insourcing, according to the second interpretation, shares some characteristics of a COE, particularly specialized staffing and equipment capabilities. Last, insourcing can mean a specialty firm hiring a company's employees but maintaining them in their former function. This interpretation of insourcing shares many of the benefits of outsourcing. (To some it is a special category of outsourcing.) The insourced function, according to the last meaning, improves processes and, usually, reduces expenses. To the extent that insourcing tilts the status quo in the direction of improvement, it shares many of the benefits of outsourcing—and some of the drawbacks.

Benefits

Sandra Golden of Your Staff, an HR management firm, presented to the Society for Advancement of Management (SAM) the results of a Coopers and Lybrand study on outsourcing HR administration. Golden told the group

- 70 percent of respondents said they achieved greater efficiency
- 45 percent increased the focus on product and growth
- 42 percent saved costs and administration
- 41 percent lowered overhead investment or debt
- 21 percent eased their regulatory compliance burden
- 18 percent outsourced because they could not find skilled employees

The Outsourcing Institute (1995) offers 10 top reasons for outsourcing, compiled from surveys of more than 1200 companies and ongoing work with its members. Consider their application to documentation functions. Potential drawbacks to outsourcing follow the benefits.

The top 10 reasons for outsourcing, and representative documentation applications, include

1. *Reduce or control operating costs.* This is the single most important tactical reason for outsourcing. An outside provider's lower cost structure can be a compelling short-term benefit.

- Outsourced documentation functions that apply zero-based methodology, empowered staff, and continuous measured process improvement can reduce operating costs from 25 to 60 percent, depending on the organization's existing processes.

2. *Make capital funds available.* Outsourcing can reduce the need to invest capital funds in noncore functions, making capital funds more available for core domains.

Checklist 9.2:
Top 10 Reasons for Outsourcing
☐ Reduce or control operating costs.
☐ Make capital funds available.
☐ Infuse cash.
☐ Substitute for resources not available internally.
☐ Obtain assistance with a function difficult to manage or out of control.
☐ Improve business focus.
☐ Access world-class capabilities.
☐ Accelerate reengineering benefits.
☐ Share risks.
☐ Free resources for other purposes.

- Computers, printers, scanners, and telecommunications hardware and facilities are primary capital expenses for documentation outsourcing.

3. *Infuse cash.* Transferring assets from the customer to a provider is an outsourcing option. Equipment, facilities, licensing, and other assets may be sold to the provider, resulting in a cash payment.

- Cash may be available from transferring computers, printers, scanners, and telecommunications and other hardware and licenses for documentation software.

4. *Substitute for resources not available internally.* Outsourcing can be a viable alternative to developing needed capability, either from the ground up, as in a new facility or geographic area added in a business expansion, or because internal resources are inaccessible.

- Implementing quality initiatives, such as ISO 9000, and other heavy documentation requirements may exceed available staffing capacities.

5. *Obtain assistance with a function difficult to manage or out of control.* Outsourcing does not substitute for management responsibility, but it can offer an option for addressing problematic workplace situations.

- Traditionally, documentation functions have had low visibility in their organizations (unless litigation, audits, or disaster recovery activities demand their involvement). Sometimes in a low visibility environment, management practices and work processes become static. For some, change can be intimidating. Outsourcing can introduce new performance expectations and objectivity.

6. *Improve business focus.* Outside experts can assume operational details while a company focuses on broader business issues. Implementation issues can siphon off management resources and attention.

- Unless documentation is a company's core business (for example, word processing or editorial firms), documentation supports manufacturing, engineering, or other functions. Managing an organization's documentation need not distract core leaders.

7. *Access world-class capabilities.* Outsourcing providers, because of their specialization, can bring extensive global, world-class resources to meet their customers' needs. Some of the capabilities an outsourcing partner can offer include access to new technology, tools, and techniques; better career opportunities for personnel who transition to the outsourcing provider; more structured approaches, procedures, and documentation; and a competitive advantage from expanded skills.

- World-class documentation, like other functions, is a result of highly trained personnel experienced in continuous process improvement and powerful technology, knowledgeable and skilled leadership, ready access to professional publications and conferences, and supportive career development. Outsourcing can deliver access to these capabilities.

8. *Accelerate reengineering benefits.* An outside organization that has already reengineered to world-class standards can allow a company to realize immediately the projected benefits of its own business process reengineering initiative.

- An outsourced documentation function can bring the quality tools, metrics, developed teamwork, and results that reengineering initiatives seek. Outsourcing can reduce a project's cycle time.

9. *Share risks.* Companies that outsource can become more flexible and dynamic. They can adapt better to changing opportunities.

- Major documentation streamlining efforts commonly require increased attention at their initiation, then taper off as processes improve. Outsourcing can better absorb the ups and downs without an organization paying for staffing that may be needed for just part of a year or without paying the hiring, learning curve, and severance costs of an expanding and contracting internal workforce.

10. *Free resources for other purposes.* No organization has unlimited resources. Outsourcing can permit an organization to redirect its resources from noncore business toward gaining a greater return in serving its customers.

- Core business produces revenue. Generally, documentation does not (unless it is a company's core business). Documentation for most companies is a separate administrative function, or it is produced to some extent by several employees, most of whom have primary responsibilities to make a product or provide a service to paying customers.

As just shown, organizations can benefit in many ways from outsourcing their documentation. Because of their access to large warehousing facilities and specialized software and skilled personnel, records storage and management firms for several years have provided a full range of outsourcing services. Records outsourcers include huge national firms and local companies. Firms that offer outsourcing services for policies and procedures have begun to spring up. But what are the drawbacks? What are the reasons organizations might not want to outsource their documentation activities?

Drawbacks

Company documentation, traditionally, has been a private matter. Organizations are concerned that proprietary information may get into the wrong hands. Employees believe that intimate knowledge of the organizational structure and individuals who make things happen in a company are critical to documentation processing. Company jargon, acronyms, and the details that only an insider would know could trip up outsourced staff.

Organizations proud of a long record of layoff-free operations are reluctant to risk damaging employee loyalty. They believe employees engaged in core business are the best choices for generating and processing their documentation. Employees handling documentation see outsourcing as a slap in the face, a lack of confidence in their skills and performance. Customers may be used to and enjoy good rapport with internal personnel; organizations do not want to risk damaging customer relationships.

Checklist 9.3: Considerations for Seeking Outside Assistance—Outsourcing or Insourcing Documentation Function

☐ Documentation function costs perceived to be too high

☐ No knowledge of document cost

☐ Outdated capital equipment and facilities

Further, companies question projected cost savings in light of an outside organization's incentive to create more work by charging fees according to time worked. Employees are concerned that an outsourcing firm's culture may be incompatible with their own.

The decision to outsource a documentation function should be made only after careful consideration of an organization's goals compared with the benefits and drawbacks of outsourcing. Note that some of the benefits of outsourcing may be achieved without some of the drawbacks by hiring or training an internal documentation specialist or by contracting with an outside specialist. Specialists can train staff and lead improvement efforts. The following considerations may help an organization decide whether to seek outside assistance—outsourcing or insourcing.

- Documentation function costs are perceived to be too high.

- No one knows the cost to produce an average policy or procedure or any other company document.

- Capital equipment and facilities are outdated for competitive documentation processing.

- Facilities or personnel are unavailable or inadequate to meet the company's expansion requirements.

- The documentation function is difficult to manage and processes are out of control. The company is buried in too much documentation. It takes too long to process new documents, revisions, or cancellations. It is difficult to find needed current or archived information quickly. Documentation is obsolete.

- Management is spending too much time putting out fires in the documentation function.

- Documentation staff members are using processes, technology, and tools that are inappropriate for world-class organizations.

☐ Facilities or personnel cannot meet expansion requirements

☐ Documentation function difficult to manage
- ☐ Too much documentation
- ☐ Takes too long to process documents
- ☐ Difficult to find information quickly
- ☐ Documentation is obsolete

☐ Management spends too much time putting out fires in documentation function

☐ Documentation staff use non–world-class processes, technology, and tools

☐ Career development limited for documentation specialists

☐ Takes too long to reengineer documentation function

☐ Core business diverted to writing documentation

- Career development is limited for documentation specialists.
- Reengineering the documentation function is taking too long.
- Core business staff members are being pulled away from serving the customer to writing documentation.

C. Skills

Empowerment without the skills to accomplish a goal is not empowerment at all. It is a recipe for failure. Documentation responsibilities are far ranging and can include everything from facilitating management focus groups to drafting a procedure to formatting one and from coordinating a policy for review to uploading to an on-line information storage and retrieval system. These are technical skills. No one should be given responsibility for accomplishing a goal if he or she does not have the skills to achieve it or plan the training to develop those skills.

For empowered documentation functions, technical skills are just the beginning. An organization can achieve nimbleness only if its members are skilled in decision making and team or group dynamics, for example, leadership responsibilities and communication, and the most overlooked team skill: active listening.

Functions often take group communication skills for granted. You may have seen the *Abilene Paradox,* the ageless video about mismanaged agreement. A reluctant family drives far in a hot, unairconditioned car to get ice cream that nobody wants. A faculty tortures itself in a boring go-nowhere meeting that nobody is brave enough to call off. Two people unhappily agree to marry because each thinks the other person will be devastated if he or she doesn't go through with it. A company attempts to produce a product that is unproducible, but everyone thinks everyone else is in favor of it. The point, of course, is that managing group agreement does not always come naturally. It is a learned skill.

Empowered documentation staff members know how to measure quality, whether it applies to accurate and current procedures or speedy cycle time for revising company forms.

Documentation functions planning to move from a traditional arrangement of supervisors dictating and employees following are urged to inventory employees' skills and provide training that addresses both technical and participation skills.

D. Self-Directed Teams

Hitting hard in the late 1980s and into the 1990s, in response to a shrinking, more competitive market, companies everywhere flattened their organizational structures to reduce operating costs (see Figure 9.1). At the same time, and for the same reasons, they demanded increased customer focus, higher quality work, and greater productivity. Also at the same time, employees watched waves of their colleagues—not just marginal performers—being laid off. Hard workers joined the unemployed, leaving survivors who now were expected to perform their own work as well as the tasks of those who left. The result in many firms was a personally threatening and highly stressful work environment, one that immobilized employees like deer in a headlight and dampened risk-taking and innovation.

At Hughes, the general story was no different, but included a few, more specific, challenges, especially to organizations that handled documentation. What used to be four divisions of one of the world's largest aerospace and defense electronics companies was now one sector, each division having its own practices and procedures and each S&P department, its own processes. Further, the operating functions that "owned" the products (practices and procedures) were consolidating too and were reluctant to let go of what they had—albeit obsolete. For example, four purchasing departments, each responsible for a purchasing procedures manual, were slow to standardize purchasing processes and consolidate written procedures.

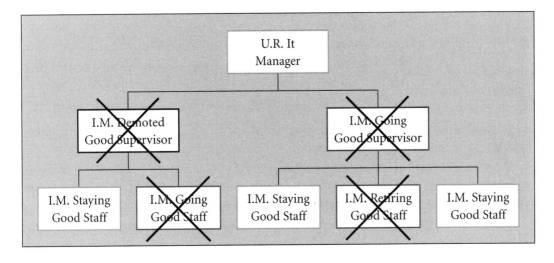

Figure 9.1. The flatter organization.

The four disparate, hierarchical central S&P departments metamorphosed into a consolidated organization of self-directed teams, which met the requirements for a flat organization—one manager with 25 direct reports, the stuff of nightmares—but also gave employees a sense of empowerment, control over their work processes, and even some dominion over their own destiny. Increased customer focus paired with better decisions, greater motivation paired with higher productivity and quality, elimination of non–value-added activities resulted in lower operating costs, and empowerment translated into less stress—for team members as well as management. The path, however, was long, crooked, and rough.

How were the self-directed S&P teams developed? What factors were important to the success of their unconventional organizational structure? Specific work situations, management styles, and team maturity dictate the ingredients and their proportions for launching other successful self-directed teams. However, the following critical elements—customers, managers and teams, goals and performance, leadership, professional development, processes, metrics, facilities, technology, and recognition—can be considered raw materials for other organizations looking to develop self-directed teams.

Customers. It is far from coincidental that focusing on customers comes first in the list of critical elements for self-directed teams. Everything else depends on understanding and knowing internal as well as external customers and other sources of need. Inaugurating self-directed documentation teams is no exception. Teams need to know they have been built to serve their customers. Transforming from traditional management to self-directed teams is hard work and requires a tremendous commitment to professional and personal growth. If flattening an organization structure makes a company more competitive by reducing operating expenses, then teams need to know this. To perform their best, members need to understand the reason behind the hardships, especially at the beginning, when stretch endurance (for example, absorbing others' workloads before processes are streamlined) seems to be tested the most.

Surveying customers (owners and users) helps self-directed teams stay directed. Communicating to customers that team members are front-line decision makers is not just a nicety; it pays off. Successful teams have managers who take the time up front to tell customers directly that team members are responsible for and have the authority to make decisions. Managers can do this best in person, either by presentations or informal meetings.

Managers and teams. Who hasn't known a team whose members were frustrated and impotent because management bypassed the team and cut deals with those outside the team? Especially in an internal documentation function, which often is considered low priority in a company, without proactive management communication, most people assume managers make the important decisions. Many treat documentation teams as merely decorative.

However, when management sends a clear message both to the team and to customers that this team means business and does business, its members begin to behave as if they really do have decision-making authority. As a result they become more responsible, focused, innovative, and productive. Managers who personally introduce team members to customers help teams build rapport and smooth the way for team decisions and operational improvements.

Finally, it is comfortable for an experienced manager to continue making presentations at high-level meetings. Growing a self-directed team, however, demands that a manager position team members in slots highly visible to customers.

☐ Regularly reviews objectives and status; refines strategies.

☐ Manager reports on objectives and status.

Leadership

☐ Determines rotating or fixed leadership.

☐ Communicates with management.

☐ Defines leadership roles and responsibilities.

☐ Conducts team meetings.

☐ Assigns subteam leaders for tasks.

☐ Requests feedback from team members.

☐ Represents department in interdepartmental committees.

☐ Shares in evaluating job candidates.

Professional Development

☐ Participates in training such as team building, team dynamics, leadership, communication, continuous measurable improvement, performance appraisal, hardware and software, proofreading, presentations, and process mapping.

☐ Cross-trains (every function has a backup).

☐ Researches and requests resources.

☐ Coaches.

☐ Extends job boundaries.

Processes

☐ Establishes ground rules.

☐ Charts current processes.

☐ Identifies value-added and non–value-added activities.

☐ Defines new and refines current processes.

☐ Defines decision-making processes.

☐ Researches and uses tools to improve processes.

☐ Benchmarks and benchtrends processes.

☐ Achieves consensus.

When the consolidated S&P department at Hughes planned a campaign to eliminate hard copy manuals, team members, not the manager, gave presentations to every internal division. Because high-level presentations were foreign to all members, a corporate communications coach was brought in to help ensure their success.

Goals and performance. Empowerment doesn't mean do the job after someone else decides what it shall be and how it shall be done. Empowered team members must participate in shaping the goals that direct their own performance.

Self-directed documentation teams flow down performance objectives from company goals to individuals' responsibilities. Say, for instance, one company goal is achieving 100 percent participation in continuous measured improvement. One of the ways a division implements this goal is speeding current plans for delivering a radar system to its customer at less cost than contracted. The company's administration function adopts the goal and lowers overhead expenses. The documentation function contributes to the savings with its flatter organizational structure by empowering self-directed teams, thereby reducing its operating costs. Documentation staff meet a zero-defects objective and reduce the expenses they would have incurred and passed on if they had to correct errors in the product operating procedures.

The seeds of a self-directed S&P team were sown in the mid-1980s with a 10-person S&P department at Hughes Ground Systems Group setting department goals. A division of about 16,000 employees, Hughes Ground Systems Group established a handful of goals that flowed down from company goals through mid-level organizations. The team developed objectives (such as a hardware standardization plan and completed training in team building), estimated completion dates, and assigned members responsible for each deliverable. After meeting weekly for a couple of months to establish the objectives, the team met quarterly to review progress toward the objectives and to revise an objective (for example, if it was no longer appropriate as written or if the responsibility for a deliverable had changed).

Objective-setting and progress meetings were highly structured and centered on progress reports (see Figure 9.2). To establish each objective, the team brainstormed, discussed merits and potential obstacles, prioritized, and assumed responsibilities. Agreement was reached through consensus, not votes. Members also researched, justified, and requested resources (dollars, personnel, facilities, and equipment) for achieving each objective. Management's primary function was to communicate the team's goals and performance to executives and other customers and to funnel resources.

Leadership. Team leadership can be rotating or fixed. Effective self-directed teams decide.

A Hughes analysts team decided first to rotate leadership monthly. After a couple of months, it switched to fixed, choosing a team leader for a six-month term, which team members later extended to a year. The support team, comprised of members responsible for word processing, secretarial, and clerical support, decided on rotating leadership weekly, then changed it to monthly. The forms team chose a leader for the year. Each leader participated with the department manager in a combined weekly team leader meeting, communicating upward, downward, and across teams; solving problems; and making decisions. A representative from each

Metrics
- ☐ Researches and develops metrics for processes.
- ☐ Maintains metrics.
- ☐ Publicizes metrics.
- ☐ Refines metrics.

Facilities
- ☐ Researches and requests room arrangements to support team structure.
- ☐ Requests ergonomics consultation.
- ☐ Researches and requests modification of lighting, furniture, and equipment to support processes.

Technology
- ☐ Researches and requests standardized hardware and software.
- ☐ Develops and implements conversion plans.
- ☐ Researches, requests, and maintains library of technology publications.

Recognition

☐ At department staff meetings, acknowledges member kindnesses and accomplishments.

☐ Approves responses to employee suggestion program.

☐ Dispenses "at-a-persons."

☐ Applies for team awards.

☐ Publicizes accomplishments in newsletters.

of the S&P work teams participated in the other teams' regular meetings and reported to his or her own team, which was critical in a documentation function, where many hands touch the same piece of work (see Figure 9.3). For example, analysts were considering changes to on-line screens, which document uploaders needed input.

Using the Joiner Associates *The Team Handbook* (Scholtes 1988), each team defined the roles and responsibilities of its leaders and assigned tasks to ad hoc subteam leaders. A key to each leader's effectiveness was specifically requesting feedback from members at each meeting. Team leaders also represented their teams regularly in interdepartmental committees. Leaders shared in many other traditional management activities, including evaluating candidates for job openings.

Professional development. Declaring an organization a team does not make it so. Just because members have been on umpteen committees in their careers does not mean they will automatically function effectively as a group. Sometimes, people need to learn different ways of looking at teams. Training helps.

Empowered, self-directed documentation teams are trained in key group processes and technical skills, such as team building; team dynamics; leadership; communication; continuous measured improvement; performance evaluation; tools, such as hardware and software; editing; word processing; proofreading; presentations; and process mapping. To be able to satisfy customer's needs, yet maintain a trim organization, empowered teams cross train members. Every function has a backup. The team assigns responsibility to a member to research training resources, such as courses, publications, and videotapes. Team leaders learn coaching techniques for optimum performance. And teams recognize the value of extending job boundaries to familiarize employees with new situations and skills they may need to meet planned objectives. In this chapter's section on Training (F), each of these elements of professional development is discussed further.

Processes. Successful self-directed teams, and traditional groups too, establish ground rules for productive meetings. They use metrics to chart current processes and target performance. They look for ways to eliminate routine

S&P Objectives Progress Report

Objective Task	Responsibility	Estimated Completion Date
4. Publicize Videotex system		
4.1 Brainstorm media	LB, AL, LH, NM	Completed
4.2 Consult with [computing support organization] for roll-out schedule	AL, SF	Completed
4.3 Research feasibility, including expense, staffing, implementation strategies	LB, AL, LH, NM	Completed
4.4 Develop preferred strategies	LB, AL, LH, NM	2/15
4.5 Present strategies for S&P consensus	LH	2/21
4.6 Develop milestones	LB, AL, LH, NM	2/21
4.7 Present report to [director]	AE	2/24
4.8 Report progress to S&P	LH, AE	2/28
5.		
5.1		
5.2		

Figure 9.2. S&P objectives progress report.

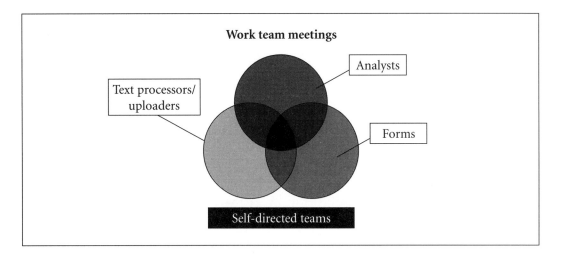

Figure 9.3. Cross team communication.

but unnecessary activities, then use tools to improve processes. Another critical element related to processes is defining decision making.

Clear ground rules make sense for teams. Take meetings, for example. Team meetings are expensive; even a few minutes of delay costs money. An effective and enjoyable technique that most teams agree to encourages members to be on time. At the start of each meeting, an inexpensive piggy bank is placed on the conference table. Late members pay a fine (usually a quarter, but some teams prefer a dollar). When the project is complete, or after a specified time period, the team spends the money on lunch. For this technique to work, the team must reach consensus on adopting it, and then allow no exceptions.

The article in Figure 9.4 emphasizes the benefits of well-managed meetings.

Ground rules for self-directed teams can include "Everyone must participate." That means no team member may merely go along for the ride and let colleagues make important decisions. Another ground rule is "Tell the truth." When a process is not working well, each team member is responsible for attending to it. Ignoring process snags delays solutions or steers a team down an unproductive path. Other ground rules borrowed from seminar participation apply to self-directed team meetings: "Show courtesy to colleagues," "Share your experience," and "Stay on topic."

To implement continuous measured improvement, team members first must examine the current processes to identify those that add value to their product or service and the ones that do not. For example, the Hughes S&P department, with a quality assurance facilitator, traced the cycle time for producing a hard copy practice. First, the team flowcharted all activities involved in producing the document. Then it estimated the number of hours for each activity, such as word processing or filing the master. If an activity was essential to producing the practice according to quality, cost, and schedule requirements, the team drew the hours for the activity above the axis. If eliminating the activity did not affect the requirements, the process fell below the axis. The team resisted categorizing an activity that was "nice to have" with the essential ones. The process charting activity opened eyes. Surprised to learn that some of the most time-consuming activities

---

Checklist 9.5: Guidelines for Conducting a Productive Meeting

☐ Decide if the potential results are worth the cost.

☐ Identify the fewest participants needed to accomplish the goal.

☐ Draft an agenda.

☐ State the nature of the meeting.

☐ Establish ground rules.

☐ Encourage participation.

☐ Summarize.

☐ Draft minutes.

What time is it? Time for your next meeting? Maybe you just came out of one. Or maybe you're in one right now and you have no idea what's being discussed. If so, now would be a good time to look up and nod. OK—continue reading.

Chances are you spend a good deal of your day in meetings. Yes, they cost time. But have you ever stopped to figure out how much money they cost?

Think of one of your recent meetings. Jot down the

- Number of participants

- Hours spent preparing for, attending, and then reporting on the meeting

- Average hourly salary for participants plus 40 percent to 50 percent for labor burden

Multiply these three numbers to find out the approximate cost of the meeting. It's not cheap. Good meetings identify challenges, speed communication, and spawn solutions. Bad meetings waste time and discourage—even alienate—participants. That's why it's a good idea to follow these simple guidelines for conducting a good, productive meeting.

- *Decide if the potential results are worth the cost.* Do this before you schedule the meeting.

- *Identify the fewest participants needed to accomplish the goal.*

- *Draft an agenda.* Include the goal of the meeting, presenters, and allotted start and stop times for each item. Distribute the agenda (use e-mail if available) before a scheduled meeting to allow participants to prepare for it. Even if the meeting is ad hoc for only a few people, take a few moments to establish an agenda, then stick to it.

- *State the nature of the meeting.* Clearly communicate whether the meeting is scheduled to convey information, generate ideas, or make decisions. Few work events are more discouraging than meetings where you expect to make a decision, only to find out you are on the receiving end of a data dump.

- *Encourage participation.* Call participants out individually if they haven't contributed and ask their opinion. Be prepared for disagreement. If the meeting's goal was easy to achieve, you probably wouldn't need the meeting. Listen.

- *Summarize.* Clearly define decisions and action items. Be sure that everyone understands his or her action items.

- *Draft minutes.* If a meeting is worth holding, it is worth recording. Minutes prevent misunderstandings. Include action items and individuals responsible for them. Spell out a reason for attendees to review the minutes.

Source: Normand L. Frigon, Harry K. Jackson, Jr., and Adrienne S. Escoe, "Meetings—Spawning Ground or Sewer?" *The Escoe/Bliss Insider for World Class Systems and Procedures.* Summer, 1996. Used with permission.

Figure 9.4. Meetings: Spawning ground or sewer?

(for example, stapling a cover sheet) contributed nothing to the practice, team members became receptive to changing the process. Identifying value-added and non–value-added activities proved very useful. If an activity was unneeded, it was discarded. As a result, refining the existing process yielded about a 45 percent reduction in processing practices.

During the course of charting a process, a self-directed team is empowered to add new processes or activities when critical gaps are discovered and to revise or resequence current ones. How does the team do that?

The scope of this book excludes detailed discussion of the variety of continuous measured improvement techniques, most born in the quality assurance community. You can learn more about these techniques by consulting a general handbook on quality or participating in meetings of ASQ or other organizations that are devoted to quality. An empowered self-directed team, however, is familiar with the most popular techniques and knows where to find more information or engage others to help. The basics are collect, record, and analyze data; identify important discrepancies; find the root causes of the discrepancies; and fix and prevent the discrepancies.

Another useful tool is benchmarking to discover best processes elsewhere (and benchtrending to anticipate future ones). The S&P team talked with policies and practices representatives from several companies to learn alternate strategies to accomplish the same objectives.

Self-directed teams early on define decision-making processes: Will it be by consensus or vote? What is the difference? Smart teams understand the power of consensus, which does not necessarily mean agreement. When a group is stuck on a particularly controversial issue team facilitators wisely ask, "Is there anyone who can't live with it?" They don't ask, "Does everyone agree." They say, "You don't have to love it. You simply have to be able to accept it and work with it." With those words, peer pressure alone often dissolves deadlocks.

Consensus usually brings buy-in and, in the best case, commitment. Where documentation functions merge (for example, in a company restructuring), staff members may disagree on writing style, format, and many other elements with which they have become familiar. Making decisions based on consensus, not votes, helps unify a team.

Metrics. Say *metrics* to beginning teams, and you see eyes roll and voices sigh. Overburdened employees balk at adding tasks, even if the activity ultimately reduces workload. Depending on requirements, documentation teams keep metrics on customer satisfaction, defect rates, currency, cycle time, volume, and cost. Metrics need not be elaborate. Simple tallying (such as for proofreading errors) or counting (such as the number of documents or number of pages) usually suffices. Spreadsheet software, such as Excel (Microsoft Office) or Lotus 1-2-3 (Lotus SmartSuite), is easy to use and creates charts for showing data and demonstrating progress.

Clear responsibility for researching, developing, and maintaining metrics is characteristic of successful self-directed teams. Publicizing progress via metrics is important too to encourage teams when self-direction gets difficult. Some organizations post monthly metrics in a well-traveled corridor both to acknowledge team accomplishments and to share ideas with other teams. Metrics are like mirrors. You do not always like what you see, but a clear picture can stimulate action. The best metrics continue to evolve; they do not stagnate. Teams review the appropriateness of the charts regularly and revise them to keep them useful. See Chapter 5 for more about documentation metrics.

Facilities. Typically, when they are told that rearranging facilities can support team processes, people say they have no funding for it. However, the benefits from team-friendly facilities often outweigh the costs.

Office arrangement can facilitate intrateam communication. At Hughes Ground Systems Group, the S&P department investigated the effect facilities had on team processes and justified a few fairly inexpensive changes. Department members relocated a door so team members' offices surrounded a small office that housed a central printer, bulletin board, and coffee machine. They did not recreate the Taj Mahal, but did speed informal decision making and improve productivity (see Figure 9.5). The department was able to pay for the remodeling and for ergonomic improvements by eliminating several individual printers and transferring depreciation costs to other departments. A team member volunteered to consult with a representative from the safety and health office and learned to conduct an ergonomics audit of the department. The result was egg crate fixtures that reduced glare on computer screens, loop-and-hook fasteners that provided earthquake protection for expensive hardware, and desks raised for two tall staff members. The potential dollar savings from these three improvements were unknown, but people enjoyed the increased comfort and peace of mind.

Technology. Self-directed teams research and justify standardized hardware and software such as computers, peripherals (printers and scanners), and programs (see Chapter 4). To maintain customer service and avoid costly rework, teams develop and implement conversion plans. To promote staff

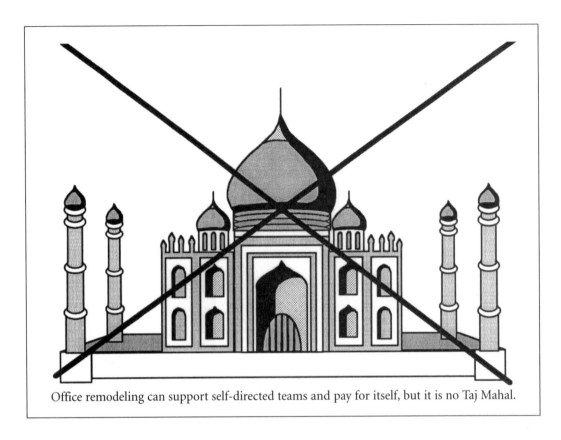

Office remodeling can support self-directed teams and pay for itself, but it is no Taj Mahal.

Figure 9.5. No Taj Mahal.

development, team members research, request, and maintain a library of publications focused on documentation technology (see the Training section in this chapter).

Recognition. If you think acknowledging kindnesses to begin each department staff meeting is hokey, think again. Particularly when self-directed teams form from consolidated organizations, every act that allies people works toward speeding process improvement, or at least toward reducing expensive divisiveness. Self-directed teams are authorized to approve recommendations in an employee suggestion program, even minor improvements, as shown by the following situation.

An organization issued an official performance improvement suggestion about a typo, a reversed closing parenthesis mark in a published bulletin. This was "trivial," they said.

The self-directed team said, "Thank you for letting us know."

Why did the team respond that way? For one, any defect, no matter how small, that slips through a documentation system indicates a process gap. If the system is not fixed, the next defect could be a major one; perhaps something that violates a regulatory requirement. Second, by acknowledging all improvement suggestions, team members adopt an attitude of constantly thinking improvement.

Other ways teams recognize performance are applying for company-sponsored team awards, dispensing "at-a-persons," publicizing accomplishments in company and division newsletters, and getting compensation based partly on team performance. Xerox Corporation celebrates an annual Teamwork Day, where successful teams go on stage and report their improvements. Events through the day are satellite-broadcast to several cities in which the corporation has facilities. Hughes Aircraft Company and many other organizations award prizes to teams that improve processes significantly. Generally, either the team submits its entry or a manager nominates the team. Managers and team leaders set the tone; they encourage team members to relate others' good deeds and share customers' commendations. Teams catch "at-a-person fever." They catch people doing things right (see Figure 9.6).

The documentation streamlining team of The Aerospace Corporation, whose case study for streamlining their policies and practices is presented in Chapter 2, structured themselves using several guidelines, as follows.

- Identify biggest obstacles to streamlining Policies and Practices, causes, and solutions (fishbone diagram).

- Establish the composition of work teams.

- Hold productive meetings

 —Give advance notice of each meeting, with specific agenda items listed (e-mail, fax, or hard copy) and participants' preparation—for example, to confer with their management or staff for ideas.

 —State what participants should bring to the meeting.

 —Include participants' immediate managers on the courtesy copies, especially for the list of members attending and those not.

 —Assign a scribe to take minutes, including agenda and action items for the next meeting.

 —Assign a facilitator (for example, a quality assurance person) to keep the meeting and the leader on track.

 —Establish due dates for assignments.

At department staff meetings, self-directed teams acknowledge
member kindnesses and accomplishments.

Figure 9.6. Recognition.

—Designate team membership. Include each functional area, corporate
documentation staff, perhaps bargaining-unit representative, and an
executive for the kickoff meeting. Perhaps plan for a team photo in
the company's newsletter (helps impart value to the project).

—Develop a process for team members' alternates.

—Establish consensus versus voting decision making.

—Define tools for starting and ending on time (for example, piggy
bank for latecomers, with luncheon to divide the bounty).

E. Roles and Responsibilities

Without clearly defined roles and responsibilities, documentation functions
can waste much time participating in ineffective meetings, challenged performance evaluations, and rework.

Teams frequently initiate projects by defining roles of the leader, facilitator, and scribe (minute-taker). Many teams, however, fail to outline the roles and responsibilities of other participants. Focus groups assembled for writing procedures and instructions and teams for documentation system improvement are no exceptions. The most effective groups define clearly at the start of the project, work year, or other interval the expectations held for each member and the consequences of failing to meet them. Time spent defining roles and responsibilities is time spent well. Roles and responsibilities clearly defined is empowering. *The Team Handbook* (Scholtes 1988) is a useful resource, spelling out ingredients for a team's success, where clear roles and responsibilities are a primary component. A successful team must have

- Clear goals
- An improvement plan
- Clearly defined roles and responsibilities
- Clear communication
- Behaviors that benefit the whole team
- Well-defined decision processes
- Balanced participation
- Established ground rules
- An awareness of group process
- Use of a scientific approach

In just hours, the Capistrano (California) Unified School District's Food Services Department developed solid work objectives for the year by mixing these ingredients into its leadership council meetings. The San Mateo County Probation Department and Monterey County Sheriff's Department did the same in a brief workshop. Hughes Aircraft Company's Ground Systems Group S&P department issued a *The Team Handbook* (Scholtes 1988) to each team member and paid particular attention to clarifying participants' roles and responsibilities.

> **Checklist 9.6: Ingredients for Team Success**
>
> ☐ Clear goals
> ☐ Improvement plan
> ☐ Clearly defined roles and responsibilities
> ☐ Clear communication
> ☐ Behaviors that benefit the whole team
> ☐ Well-defined decision processes
> ☐ Balanced participation
> ☐ Established ground rules
> ☐ An awareness of group process
> ☐ Use of a scientific approach

A few years prior to forming self-directed teams, this organization developed performance criteria upon which to evaluate employees. Structured according to performance elements described on the company's performance planning and appraisal form, the criteria were created expressly for S&P analysts and text processing and secretarial staff. At the time, the department had been operating for about a quarter of a century without the benefit of significant quality or process improvement initiatives. This was also a time when personal computers were replacing dedicated word processing equipment and new managers came into the department with fairly revolutionary ideas about quality, performance, and accountability. The performance criteria were keyed to *Meets company standards,* which was the third of five assessment options, from *Does not meet requirements* to *Far exceeds requirements* (see Appendices A and B).

F. Training

People are like bananas: They are either green and growing or ripe and rotting.

World-class documentation functions cannot afford to rest on old knowledge. Change is everywhere: technology, quality initiatives, competition. The old paradigm was that staff became trained for a career path—period. That paradigm no longer applies, especially to a successful, empowered workforce.

The Hughes S&P work teams participated in several kinds of training, including formal classroom, self-training, cross training, coaching and one-on-one training, and extended job boundaries.

Classroom training included the company's cascaded continuous measurable improvement (cmi) workshop (the acronym lowercased in all documentation because of the company's emphasis on improvement as a way of life, not a program). First, managers were team trained by their directors or division heads and staff members from the company's training department. Next, each manager team-trained his or her staff members with a member from the company's quality assurance function. The eight-hour workshop for staff covered cmi basics. The curriculum also included cmi benefits and processes, metrics, process maps, working environments conducive to initiating improvements, empowerment, team dynamics, benchmarking, and problem solving with quality tools. Every S&P staff member participated in the cmi workshop.

Other classroom training for work team members covered standardized hardware and software—a standard desktop computer platform and standardized software were adopted across the department—including word processing, communications, drawing, publishing, presentations, project scheduling, database, and spreadsheet. Support personnel received specialized training in networks and the mainframe-based information storage and retrieval system.

Depending on individual objectives, staff members participated in a wide variety of other classes and seminars, including creativity, time management, goal setting, performance evaluation, meetings management, and many others. Team leaders participated in organizational change and team communication classes. Staff members were trained in proofreading.

Self-training consisted of books and videos recommended by managers, team leaders, or colleagues, or they were individuals' selections. The department produced a routing slip personalized for each employee, who fastened the slip to journal articles, news clips, and other pertinent information to share with colleagues. At a team member's suggestion, the department established a small technical library and subscribed to leadership, documentation, and software-oriented publications.

To develop and multiply employee skills, at least one person was cross trained in each major process performed within the department. That way, a minimum number of staff members could achieve department objectives. Cross training helped the department continue to serve its customers during staff leaves of absence and the work load peaks and valleys common to documentation functions. For example, an analyst was trained in basic network processes to fill in for a vacationing support team member. A forms administrator did editing when several functions updated all of their procedures at one time, swamping the analysts. By the end of the first year of consolidation, every process had a trained backup.

It has been said that the function of a coach is to take people from where they are to where they want to be. With good coaching, people tend to reduce their mistakes and unproductive habits of the past and succeed in creating a vision of the future. Through training in coaching, team leaders joined managers in assuming the coach's role, in everything from following team meeting ground rules to performance appraisal and planning discussions.

One-on-one training is an important but often overlooked training method. Empowered organizations not only rely on one-on-one training, but tie it to company objectives and record it. The quality assurance manager of a spring manufacturer seeking ISO 9001 registration is responsible for training a group of employees to draft work instructions for all functions. The one-on-one training sessions are paced to each employee's learning speed and avoid the disruption that group training would bring to the production line. However, because one-on-one training sessions tend to be

---

Checklist 9.7: One-on-One Training to Write Work Instructions

☐ Describe the big picture.

☐ Explain reason for training.

☐ Describe trainee's responsibilities.

☐ Communicate that you don't expect perfect spelling, perfect grammar, and so on. Use word processing expert to format and fix.

☐ Provide a reference (finished) document.

☐ Show examples: what "deliverable" should look like.

☐ Give or ask for reasonable schedule.

☐ State clearly times trainer is available for questions and help.

---

informal, it is easy to overlook important points. The manager developed a list of considerations to help.

- Describe the big picture.

- Don't assume the trainee knows why he or she is being trained. Give the reasons.

- Describe the trainee's responsibilities.

- Make it easy. If you can, communicate that you don't expect perfect spelling, grammar, and so on. Use a word processing expert to format and fix the instructions later.

- Provide a reference (finished) document.

- Show examples of what the employee's "deliverable" should look like.

- Give or ask for a reasonable schedule.

- State clearly when the trainer is available for questions and help.

People learn by doing, which sometimes is the most effective kind of training. In the GSG S&P department, a doubting department secretary, who was responsible for developing and coordinating organization charts for the division, became the leader of a successful cross-functional team chartered to improve chart processing cycle time. Previously, support staff were invisible to major improvement teams. Not only did the staff member learn a lot about team dynamics, but the entire department learned about the importance of including everyone involved in a process.

G. Accountability

Accountability for documentation begins with customers and other sources of need. People who are responsible for world-class documentation develop performance goals to meet the needs of legal requirements, external customers, users, subject matter owners, and certification auditors and examiners. Direct supervisors are customers, too. Accountability closes the loop between sources of need and an organization's performance. The best organizations document their need-driven goals, and all functions within the organization document operational objectives that flow from the goals. In multilevel organizations, company goals translate into division goals, then department objectives, team objectives, and finally, individual performance objectives. Each level's performance is measured against its goals or objectives. If performance falls short, the performing organization, team, or individual takes corrective action or justifies nonperformance. At each level, performers answer to customers and other sources of need. Consequences are expected at each level both for meeting goals (for example, commendations, positive performance evaluations, and career growth) and for falling short of them (such as corrective action and progressive discipline).

An empowered documentation department drafts its objectives at the beginning of the evaluation period. At Hughes Aircraft Company's Aerospace and Defense Sector, S&P department employees studied their division's goals, which flowed down from company goals. One of the higher level goals was to make the company an excellent place in which to work. After flowing down to S&P staff, an analyst team goal translated into the practice of "catching employees doing something right" and rewarding them. Team leaders received coupons to a local fast food restaurant to give to team members on-the-spot for actions that contributed to the well-being of the team. The individual who coordinated the coupons assumed that responsibility, and a time for developing it, at an earlier goal-setting meeting. Quarterly meetings, where performance is reviewed, facilitated accountability for meeting goals. And the individual's annual formal performance appraisal included the goal and his or her performance to it.

Another example started with the company's goal on quality products and services. The Hughes Ground Systems Group S&P department flowed this goal into the division's defect-free practices manual. The department reviewed defect metrics monthly and watched them reach zero as staff members trained in proofreading techniques. For its accomplishments, the department won an award for world-class documentation. And individual employees were held accountable for their part. Achieving zero defects was an individual objective as well.

H. Evaluation

Empowerment requires accountability. And accountability is impossible without performance evaluation.

Evaluation is a powerful tool for focusing a team's energies. It furnishes critical feedback and data for continued measured improvement. Hughes established a companywide performance and appraisal planning system around five elements—documentation, communication, goal-setting, employee development, and active participation—which the S&P consolidation and improvement work teams modified for team use. Each element of the Hughes system is described briefly followed by the process the work teams used to customize the system for team performance evaluation.

Checklist 9.8: Elements of Team Performance Evaluation
☐ Documentation
☐ Communication
☐ Goal-setting
☐ Employee development
☐ Active participation
☐ Flexibility for rating in a team environment
☐ Team participation in appraising performance
☐ Rater weighting modifiable according to maturity of the system
☐ Ratings compatible with company systems
☐ Familiarity of form

- *Documentation.* A four-page form for salaried employees describes performance in specified areas of work. The S&P work teams added a fifth page to compile and compute team ratings.

- *Communication.* Discussions centered on the described performance tell employees how well their performance is meeting goals and standards.

- *Goal-setting.* Team leaders, supervisors, and employees collaborate to establish reachable work objectives for the next evaluation period.

- *Employee development.* Team leaders, supervisors, and employees identify competencies to strengthen or develop and resources such as training courses to help them achieve the competencies.

- *Active participation.* Active involvement throughout the performance appraisal and planning process produces the most valid information and employees' commitment to achieving agreed-upon goals.

Soon after the work teams were organized, it became clear that the company's standard performance appraisal and planning form was inadequate for evaluating performance in a self-directed team environment. Individual evaluations, with their implications for comparisons among individual performers, it was thought, could result in individual competitiveness and work against team objectives. For example, when individuals are rewarded for their own accomplishments, and not for the team's, they may be tempted not to communicate or share ideas and solutions.

The work teams sponsored a small subteam to benchmark with other local companies known for progressive administrative processes. The subteam members also consulted with other Hughes divisions to find other groups that may have been developing team performance evaluations. They benchmarked with City National Bank, Farmers Insurance, the Los Angeles Air Force Base, Locomotion Inc., Nissan Corporation, Northrop Corporation, the Port of Los Angeles, The Aerospace Corporation, Toyota Motors, TRW, Xerox Corporation, and three Hughes divisions: Electro-Optical Systems, Surface Systems, and Hughes Space and Communications Company.

At the time, the team found that only three of the benchmarked sources had a form to evaluate team performance: Xerox, Surface Systems division of Hughes Aircraft Company, and Hughes Space and Communications.

Work team leaders reviewed form samples, reached consensus on content and format, voted on a rating scale and weighting (when consensus could not be reached), and created a team performance evaluation form modified from the company's standard form. Advantages of the modified form were flexibility, team participation, modifiable rater weighting, compatibility with companywide compensation and employee relations systems, and familiarity.

- *Flexibility for rating in a team environment.* The new form could be modified to accept performance ratings from an employee's supervisor, team leader, manager, or peer. Each work team decided who it wanted to rate team members. If one team decided to have its team leader and peers rate performance, then the performance of each member of that team was rated by the same raters. (Company personnel systems at the time required the function's supervisor of record to sign the form.) Because the form was computerized, it could be revised easily for each team. Ratings from internal customers were later added to the process.

- *Team participation in appraising performance.* Work teams participated fully by describing performance elements and rating them for each team member. They submitted a form for each team peer to the manager, who compiled comments and ratings. Several members asked to remain anonymous in their peer rating.

- *Rater weighting could be modified according to the maturity of the team.* At the time the new form was introduced, the S&P work teams were in various stages of maturity—from the "green" support team that had been established for a short time to the self-directed analyst team that had been working together for many months. The newest team weighted the manager's, team leader's, and peers' rating nearly equally, whereas the analyst team assigned 15 percent to the manager's rating. The closer the team members were to self-direction, the more they trusted their own judgment in rating their peers.

• *Resulting letter ratings were compatible with compensation and employee relations systems.* Although the route to determining letter ratings was non-standard for the company, each employee's overall performance rating fit within the company's compensation and employee relations systems, thus empowering the teams to improve the documentation function processes.

• *Familiarity.* The new form departed slightly from the company standard. *Team, team member,* and *team leader* were incorporated into the evaluation form and process. Because the new form was similar to the company's standard form, the only training needed was in entering and computing weighted ratings and peer evaluation narratives.

The team performance planning and appraisal form was a hybrid between the company's performance reporting requirements for individual employees and a company form yet to be created expressly for evaluating teams. But it was the best way the teams at the time could evaluate their own performance without compromising the company's compensation and employee relations systems.

Appraisal and planning discussions were held between each employee, his or her work team leader, and the department manager.

How did empowerment work for the S&P function? In months, not years, four discrete documentation departments, each representing a division of several thousand employees, merged. The new function consolidated the practices manuals, forms, and approval authority systems of each division. Staff members agreed upon a common writing style. They reduced documentation cycle time, volume, and expenses and achieved zero defects. They made documentation accessible to employees through an on-line information storage and retrieval system. Team members learned to work collaboratively, strengthen leadership and communication skills, give presentations to senior managers, and expand their professional skills, such as familiarity with cutting-edge documentation technology. Other indicators of successful empowerment were increased staff creativity (evidenced by the number and quality of skyrocketed, company-issued performance improvement and cost improvement certificates) and a flattened management structure (supervisor to staff ratio of 1/25). Chapter 5 presents improvement points of focus and metrics for a documentation COE.

PART IV

Information Tools

APPENDIX A

Performance Criteria for Systems and Procedures Analysts

The following describes the minimum performance criteria for *Meets Company Standards*. This document is not all-inclusive; but is provided to summarize and baseline performance standards.

Quality

Delivering a product or service that meets the needs of customers and the goals of the organization. Providing a product or service that satisfies customers. One's work reflects dependability, consistency, accuracy, thoroughness, and pride in workmanship—exemplifying that one has given one's best effort to the task. Finished products (such as directive documents, internal memos, and research analyses) are accurate.

Performance to Schedule

Meets targeted deadlines. Exercises good time management so (1) individual doesn't have to readjust schedule, and (2) individual doesn't experience last-minute time crunch, which can result in the inability to take on other tasks and assignments. Balances workload so individual can manage long-term projects (such as restructuring a manual or designing a system), as well as routine tasks, paper flow, and the preparation of directive material (such as editing documents, preparing coordinations, and interfacing with division representatives). Understands the nature of the profession and that an individual works to complete the job to quality standards even it if requires working hours in excess of the standard work week.

Cost-Effectiveness

Compares costs prior to recommending purchases. Collects and uses data to determine the most cost-effective means of acquiring materials and services. Identifies key factors in work efficiency, then looks for ways to improve efficiency without sacrificing quality or good customer service practices. Recommends expenditures acknowledging short- as well as long-term impact on the department.

Technical Contribution

Contributes innovative and practical solutions to business challenges. Keeps informed of and communicates information about tools of the trade, such as editing, analysis, and search software; e-mail; and training materials. Seeks out technical solutions from best practices in other organizations, such as departments, divisions, and groups.

Decision Making

Makes decisions that are based upon relevant facts, are well thought out, and reflect good judgment, including

1. The best way to accomplish a task

2. Asking for assistance from other personnel when given or having assumed an overwhelming task or assignment

3. Assisting customers in person or over the telephone on problems such as setting priorities for reviewing directive documents

Has working knowledge of problem-solving processes and the ability to generate options. Demonstrates resourcefulness by calling upon managers, colleagues, or other sources for assistance. Researches, analyzes, and recommends alternatives for resolving difficult situations. Handles customer requests directly whenever possible. Determines when a coordination, editing, publication, or administrative procedure requires modification to meet customer or organization needs (that is, goes outside established routines).

Knowledge

Demonstrates knowledge in each of the following areas.

1. Management principles and practices
2. Operating systems, procedures, forms, office equipment
3. On-line systems application
4. Business English, particularly writing, editing, and proofreading
5. Ability to identify and locate subject matter expertise

Draws upon past professional experience as well as education to contribute to the department's products and services. Uses knowledge to select best means of meeting a business objective, project, or assignment. Takes responsibility for developing or modifying systems applications, designing reporting media, and preparing and publishing brochures, manuals, bulletins, and other documents. May be assigned and is expected to take responsibility for surveillance, maintenance, and coordination of management or operations control system.

Personal Productivity

Demonstrates concern for and supports the role of S&P by participating fully in department-sponsored programs and services, such as demonstrations, presentations, improvement teams, and Corporate S&P functions. Sets challenging goals that build upon one's current level of competency. Goals reflect job-related issues, the process of work, and the end result. Individual is punctual. Attendance is consistent and reliable to ensure person (1) is dependable and available, and (2) is at work during the times S&P customers expect staff to be at work. Demonstrates ability to prioritize work assignments and reduce non–value-added time. Demonstrates ability to take initiative on new projects. Continually evaluates projects for improvement. Needs minimal direction and supervision follow-through.

Communication

Demonstrates knowledge of effective oral and written communication techniques for varied situations. Individual shows flexibility and professional business manners in adjusting communication approach to people he or she encounters. Uses tact and courtesy in communicating with customers, colleagues, and managers. Participates in staff meetings and other forums that are a vehicle for communicating information regarding the progress and direction of the department. Escalates problems and issues in a timely manner (that is, no surprises when a project or task promises to miss a deadline). Communicates to other staff and to supervisors to keep them apprised on current issues. Exercises professional and sound judgment in the use of written communication. Using past professional experience and education, demonstrates ability to communicate in a coherent, professional manner to employees at all levels, including frequent contracts with division, Group, and Corporate staff managers. Demonstrates competency in written communication by less need for clarification following the publication of documents. Is effective in interpretive and persuasive contacts with supervisors and managers regarding S&P analysis, development, and communication, and assists management, when requested, in the preparation of formal analyses and presentations.

Ethics

Demonstrates honesty in all aspects of the job. Upholds the Company's ethics policies. Recognizes one's own abilities and is honest about one's capabilities and limitations—"truth in advertising." Exercises discretion in the work environment.

APPENDIX B

Performance Criteria for Systems and Procedures Text Processor and Secretarial Staff

The following criteria define the work standards for *Meets Company Standards.* This is not an all-inclusive document, but is provided to summarize and baseline performance standards. The performance criteria are cumulative, that is, criteria listed for the Secretary position also apply to the Text Processor Senior and Specialist positions, whenever separate criteria are assigned to those positions.

Quality

Delivering a product or service that meets the needs of the customer and the goals of the organization. Providing a product or service that satisfies customers. One's work reflects dependability, consistency, accuracy, thoroughness, and pride in workmanship—exemplifying that one has given one's best effort to the task. Finished products (such as word processing, typing, copying, preparing distributions, filing, and so on) are accurate. Proofreads own copy for accuracy, format, and consistency and makes corrections as needed.

Performance to Schedule

Secretary. Meets due dates and requirements of assigned tasks. When setting own due dates, meets the committed dates. Provides realistic estimate of time to complete an assignment.

Text Processor Senior. Demonstrates skills in planning ahead and managing time to meet the schedule while working for multiple staff and projects. Responds well to priority changes while accomplishing tasks for multiple staff and projects.

Text Processor Specialist. Maintains section staff schedules, that is, keeps track of attendance, meetings, and other staff events.

Cost-Effectiveness

Secretary. Compares costs prior to purchasing supplies. Collects and uses data to determine the most cost-effective means of acquiring materials and services.

Text Processor Senior. Accurately tracks expenses and statistical data. Maintains accurate and reasonable inventory of office supplies.

Text Processor Specialist. Identifies key factors in work efficiency, then looks for ways to improve efficiency without sacrificing quality or good customer service practices.

Decision Making

Secretary. Makes decisions that are within the scope of one's responsibilities including

- The best way to accomplish a task
- Asking for assistance from other text processor or secretarial personnel on an overwhelming task or assignment
- Assisting customers in person or over the telephone on problems, such as requesting manuals or directing customers to the person or organization that can help them

Text Processor Senior. Researches, analyzes, and recommends alternatives for resolving difficult situations.

Text Processor Specialist. Determines the types of documents and information needed to maintain a project. Determines when an office procedure requires modification to meet customer or staff needs (that is, goes outside established policies). Handles customer requests directly whenever possible, to reduce cycle time.

Knowledge

Secretary. Knows Company policies and practices related to office transactions, for example, timecards, personal car mileage, HR services, and MRTs [material transfers]. Competent in operating office equipment such as typewriters, computers, fax machines, copiers, and multiple line telephones. Competent in using various computer software used in the department. Knows process of using support services, for example, Marketing Publications, Reproduction Services, Photo Lab, and Mail Services. Knows how to establish and maintain filing systems for quick retrieval of records and references.

Text Processor Senior. Maintains accurate inventory for S&P demonstrations and presentations, for example, handouts and viewgraphs.

Text Processor Specialist. Knows the administrative procedures for all S&P-sponsored projects. Has solid working knowledge of related functions, for example, Distribution Center and Product Operations Procedures [which later merged with the S&P department]. This knowledge is reflected in accurate referrals and information.

Personal Productivity

Secretary. Proactively shares job-related information with colleagues and supervisors in a timely manner. Establishes good rapport with customers to increase job efficiency. Assists other support personnel. Individual is punctual. Has consistent and reliable attendance to ensure person (1) is dependable and available, so that work assignments do not have to be reassigned to other support personnel, (2) is at work during the times S&P customers expect staff to be at work, and (3) provides department telephone coverage. Participates in job-related problem solving, such as workload appraisal and scheduling and responsibility for copying. Follows through on commitments. Proactively follows up with customers to determine quality of service provided by support staff.

Text Processor Senior and Specialist. Establishes work flow processes or files when such processes or information will improve efficiency for future needs. Maintains readily accessible files and documentation on procedural and administrative tasks. Provides logistical support to ensure that a project runs smoothly even if an analyst isn't available to help make decisions. Contributes ideas that will maintain the professional image of S&P. Gathers information to support reports, budgets, and presentations.

Communication

Secretary. Communicates in a clear, articulate, and courteous manner. Exercises good use of English (oral and written). Can diffuse angry customers to (1) resolve the issue or (2) refer the customer to an analyst or supervisor. Escalates problems or issues in a timely manner, for example, conflicts with work priorities. Proactively provides job information to colleagues and supervisors (for example, changes in mail delivery, new administrative procedures, and messages) in a timely manner. Follows up to ensure understanding. When customers call or drop in with questions, the individual responds courteously, accurately, and reflects a united S&P organization. That is, one does not respond with "I don't know anything about it." Records messages accurately and legibly and places them in message slots immediately. Hand delivers urgent messages immediately. Records assignments in writing to ensure accuracy. Takes and composes meeting minutes.

Text Processor Senior and Specialist. Initiates communication with all individuals needed to complete a quality job (for example, with other Text Processor staff, analysts and administrators, supervisors, and managers). Composes and edits routine correspondence (within the area of job responsibility) necessary to ensure smooth running of a project or administrative process.

Ethics

Honest in all aspects of the job. Maintains confidential information. Honors and handles Company Private and Sensitive information according to established procedures. Adheres to Company standards. Because Secretary and Text Processor personnel are often privy to sensitive information (such as phone messages, interoffice memos, and verbal conversations), exercises discretion and good judgment in handling such information.

Resources

The entries listed in this chapter are a sample of organizations, including their publications, and software useful for developing and managing documentation. Some, such as Internet web sites (see section B, Software), are excellent starting points for seeking additional resources. This information is provided for readers' convenience; an entry's inclusion is not an endorsement nor is an omission an indication of criticism. Expect changes in listed telephone numbers, especially area codes, e-mail addresses (they include the @ symbol), and Internet sites (which begin with http://). All information in this chapter was drawn from organizations' promotional literature, Internet sites, or correspondence originating from those sources.

A. Organizations

American Society for Quality (ASQ)
P.O. Box 3005
Milwaukee, WI 53201-3005
Tel 800-248-1946; 414-272-8575 (outside North America)
Fax 414-272-1734
E-mail asq@asq.org
Web site http://www.asq.org

National association for quality professionals and all others interested in quality information and technology. Divisions focus on 21 distinct industries and markets. Local sections. Provides training in quality audits, ISO 9000, SPC, TQM, and other initiatives. Certifies quality engineers and other quality professionals. More than 130,000 members.

ASQ Quality Press Publications Catalog
The American Society for Quality (ASQ)
Customer Service
PO Box 3066
Milwaukee, WI 53201-3066
Tel 800-248-1946; 414-272-8575 (outside North America)
Fax 414-272-1734

Nearly 100 pages of books, software, videotapes, CDs, audiotapes, and quality standards. Quality initiatives, such as ISO 9000, are well represented as are all other current quality topics.

ASQ journals: *Quality Progress, Journal of Quality Technology, Quality Engineering, Technometric,* and *Quality Management Journal.*

Association for Information and Image Management (AIIM)
1100 Wayne Avenue
Suite 1100
Silver Spring, MD 20910-5603
Tel 301-587-8202
Fax 301-587-2711
E-mail aiim@aiim.org

Association for information management professionals and providers of digital document technologies. Membership of more than 9000 is represented in 150 countries, with about 50 chapters. Actively involved in promoting interoperability and multivendor integration.

AIIM InfoShop
Association for Information and Image Management (AIIM)
More than 370 books, CDs, video and audio programs, slide shows, and disks on technology, professional development, education tools, and industry standards.

AIIM magazine: *INFORM*

AIIM fax service: *DOC.1*

**Association for Records Managers and Administrators (ARMA)
International**
4200 Somerset Drive, Suite 215
Prairie Village, KS 66208
Tel 800-422-2762; 913-341-3808 (outside North America)
Fax 913-341-3742
E-mail 76015,3151@Compuserve.com
Web site http://www.arma.org

*Organization for records and information managers. Promotes programs of
research, education, training, and networking. More than 10,000 members in
39 countries.*

Technical Publications Catalog
Association for Records Managers and Administrators (ARMA) International

*More than 30 pages of books and videotapes on records and information
management.*

ARMA international journal: *Records Management Quality.*

Society for Technical Communication (STC)
901 N. Stuart Street, Suite 904
Arlington, VA 22203-1854
Tel 703-522-4114
Fax 703-522-2075
BBS 703-522-3299
E-mail stc@tmn.com

*Worldwide association serving the technical communication profession, including
writers, editors, graphic artists and technical illustrators, translators, independent
consultants and contractors, photographers, and audiovisual specialists. Serves
19,000 members in 144 chapters.*

STC journal: *Technical Communication*

STC Policies and Procedures Professional Interest Committee (PIC)
Kevin J. Schmidt, Membership
Westinghouse Savannah River Co.
1000 Brookhaven Drive
Room 121
Aiken, SC 29803
Tel 803-644-1415
Fax 803-644-1110

STC PIC focuses on policies and procedures. 170 members.

B. Software

Many software packages listed in this section are widely available at electronics, office supply, and software retailers; through software mail order catalogs; and through the Internet. Some of the software, especially office suite, is stocked by department stores and larger discount variety stores. Suppliers of specialized software, such as for records management, demonstrate their products at exhibitions, for example, at ARMA International's annual conferences (see section A, Organizations). ASQ's *Quality Progress* publishes an annual directory of quality software (usually in April), including packages for developing metrics and documentation.

Flowcharts, Process Maps, and Organization Charts

ABC FlowCharter Micrografx: 800-671-0144; sales@micrografx.com;
     http://www.micrografx.com

allCLEAR SPSS: 800-543-2185; http://www.spss.com

Flow Charting PDQ Patton & Patton: 800-525-0082;
     sales@patton-patton.com; http://www.patton-patton.com

Org Plus Broderbund Software: 800-548-1798; http://www.broderbund.com

Procedure Design MEGA International: 800-920-MEGA;
     info@us.mega.com; http://www.mega.com

Process Charter Scitor: 415-462-4200; info@scitor.com;
     http://www.scitor.com

TopDown Flowcharter Kaetron Software: 800-938-8900; sales@kaetron.com;
     http://www.kaetron.com

Visio Visio Corporation: 800-24-VISIO [800-248-4746]; csdirect@visio.com; http://www.visio.com

9000 Maps EtQ Management Consultants: 800-354-4476; 71763,1022@compuserve.com; http://ourworld.compuserve.com/homepages/EtQHome

Forms

FORMS (FOrms Recognition and Management System) InnoTech: 817-795-4667; innotech@why.net; http://www.why.net/users/innotech

OmniForm Caere: 800-535-7226; http://www.caere.com

Layout and Publishing

Adobe FrameMaker Adobe: 408-536-6000; http://www.adobe.com

Adobe PageMaker Adobe: 408-536-6000; http://www.adobe.com

Microsoft Publisher Microsoft: 800-426-9400; http://www.microsoft.com

QuarkXPress Quark: 800-676-4575; http://www.quark.com

Office Suites

(Suite packages typically include word processing, spreadsheet, database, and presentation; some also include scheduling and contact management.)

Corel WordPerfect Suite Corel: 800-772-6735; http://www.corel.com

Lotus SmartSuite Lotus Development: 800-343-5414; http://www.lotus.com

Microsoft Office Microsoft: 800-426-9400; http://www.microsoft.com

Performance Appraisal

Employee Appraiser Austin-Hayne: 888-850-3566; solutions@austin-hayne.com; http://www.austin-hayne.com

Performance Now! KnowledgePoint: 800-727-1133; kp@knowledgepoint.com; http://www.knowledgepoint.com

Policies and Procedures

Descriptions Now! KnowledgePoint: 800-727-1133; kp@knowledgepoint.com;
   http://www.knowledgepoint.com

Instruction Writer 9000 Powerway: 800-964-9004;
   http://www.swcp.com/~helios/powerway

Policies Now! KnowledgePoint: 800-727-1133; kp@knowledgepoint.com;
   http://www.knowledgepoint.com

Policy Writer 9000 Powerway: 800-964-9004;
   http://www.swcp.com/~helios/powerway

Procedure Writer 9000 Powerway: 800-964-9004;
   http://www.swcp.com/~helios/powerway

The Complete Employee Handbook Made Easy ISBE Employers of America:
   800-728-3187; employer@employerhelp.org;
   http://www.smartbiz.com/sbs/pubs/nl5a.htm

Portable Document Format (PDF) Conversion

(Used for converting documents to share on networks and intranet applications)

Adobe Acrobat Adobe: 408-536-6000; http://www.adobe.com

Records Management

AIS-RMS Assured Information Systems: 610-459-0711

Corporate Keeper, Active Keeper Andrews Software: 800-807-2093

Cuadra STAR Cuadra Associates: 310-478-0066

extemporé Select Technologies: 208-375-7100; select@micron.net;
   http://www.selectec.com

GAIN Triadd Software: 206-481-9468; http://www.triaddsoftware.com

ImageTrax Document Control Solutions: 714-738-6131;
   http://www.doccontrol.com

RecFind GMB Support: 619-625-4663; 75054.1016@compuserve.com;
   http://www.gmb.com

Renaissance Renaissance Records Management: 303-972-4536

RMS MDY Advanced Technologies: 201-797-6676; info@mdyadvtech.com

SIMPLE Records Manager Records Center Software: 800-432-8160; info@recordsmanager.com; http://www.recordsmanager.com

Total Recall DHS Associates: 904-284-8900

TRIM TOWER Software: 703-359-4343; http://www.towersoft.com

Versatile Zasio Enterprises: 800-845-1002

Versatrac Versatrac: 800-547-8222; info@versatrac.com; http://www.versatrac.com

Storage and Retrieval

RetrievalWare Excalibur Technologies: 703/761.3700; info@excalib.com; http://www.xrs.com

TOPIC Verity: 408-541-1500; info@verity.com; http://www.verity.com

DOCS Open PC DOCS: 617-273-3800; info@pcdocs.com; http://www.pcdocs.com

Documentum RDM Enterprise Document Management System (EDMS) Documentum: 888-362-3367; info@documentum.com; http://www.documentum.com

Worldview Interleaf: 800-955-5323; i-direct@interleaf.com; http://www.ileaf.com

Web Page Development

Home Page Claris: 800-544-8554; http://www.claris.com

Internet Chameleon NetManage: 408-973-7171; info@netmanage.com; http://www.netmanage.com

Microsoft FrontPage Microsoft: 800-426-9400; http://www.microsoft.com

QuickSite DeltaPoint: 800-446-6955; DeltaPoint@aol.com; 76004.1522@compuserve.com; http://www.deltapoint.com

Web Commander Luckman Interactive: 800-711-2676; http://www.luckman.com

WebPublisher: Asymetrix: 206-462-0501; http://www.asymetrix.com

Web Site Searching

Web site addresses, called URLs (Uniform Resource Locators), change frequently. If, during a search, a URL listed in this chapter no longer can be found, go to one of the web sites listed here and type in the product or company name, or select a category listed there. You may be able to find the web site through this alternate route.

ALTA VISTA   http://www.altavista.digital.com

ELECTRIC LIBRARY   http://www.infonautics.com

EXCITE   http://www.excite.com

INFOSEEK   http://www.guide.infoseek.com

LYCOS   http://www.a2z.lycos.com

NEW RIDERS YELLOW PAGES   http://www.mcp.com/newriders/wwwyp

YAHOO!   http://www.yahoo.com

References

Abilene Paradox, adapted from the article "The Abilene Paradox: The Mismanagement of Agreement," in *Organizational Dynamics* by Jerry B. Harvey. 1974. New York: AMACOM, Screenplay by Kirby Timmons, CRM Films, 1991.

American Society for Quality Control, International Organization for Standardization, and American National Standards Institute. 1996. *Environmental Management Systems—Specification with Guidance for Use (ANSI/ISO 14001-1996)*. Milwaukee, Wisc.: ASQC.

American Society for Quality Control Standards Committee for American National Standards Committee Z-1 on Quality Assurance. 1994. *Quality Systems—Model for Quality Assurance in Design, Development, Production, Installation, and Servicing (ANSI/ASQC Q9001-1994)*. Milwaukee, Wisc.: ASQC.

Brumm, Eugenia K. 1995. *Managing Records for ISO 9000 Compliance*. Milwaukee, Wisc.: ASQC Quality Press.

The Forum Corporation. 1992. *cmi Leadership: Cascaded Training*.

Frigon, Norman L., Harry K. Jackson, Jr., and Adrienne S. Escoe. 1996. "Meetings—Spawning Ground or Sewer." *Escoe/Bliss Insider for World Class Systems and Procedures* (Summer): 2.

Hudiburg, John J. 1991. *Winning with Quality: The FPL Story*. White Plains, N.Y.: Quality Resources.

Huyink, David S. 1996. "From ISO 9000 to Total Quality Management: How ISO 9000 Makes TQM Easier." *Proceedings of ASQC's 50th Annual Quality Congress.* Milwaukee, Wisc.: ASQC.

"ISO 9000 for Quality's Sake." 1996. *Journal of Business Strategy* (September/October): 7.

Kerr, John. n.d. "But Is It Better Than Baldrige?" *An Insider's Guide to ISO 9000.* Newport Beach, Calif.: IMPAC Integrated Systems. Reprinted in *Escoe/Bliss Insider for World Class Systems and Procedures* (Summer 1996): 4.

Krell, Susan K. 1995. "Revision of Personnel Manuals: An Exercise in Futility?" *The Personnel Law Update* (November): 4.

National Institute of Standards and Technology. 1997. *Malcolm Baldrige National Quality Award 1997 Criteria for Performance Excellence.* Gaithersburg, Md.: National Institute of Standards and Technology.

The Outsourcing Institute. 1995. "Redefining the Corporation of the Future." *Fortune* (16 October): Advertising supplement.

The Rummler-Brache Group. 1987. *Cross-Functional Process Flow.*

Scholtes, Peter R. 1988. *The Team Handbook.* Madison, Wisc.: Joiner Associates.

Skupsky, Donald S. 1994. *Records Retention Procedures.* Englewood, Colo.: Information Requirements Clearinghouse.

Streetman, Kibbee. 1996. "Who Holds the Keys to Encrypted Electronic Documents?" *Technologies for Managing Information.* ARMA International, Vol. 1, No. 4 (May): 2–5.

The University of Chicago Press. 1993. *The Chicago Manual of Style.* 14th ed. Chicago: The University of Chicago Press.

Urgo, Raymond E. 1995. *Comparison Test: Non-Structured/Non-Modular Version.* Participant materials presented at the Orange Empire Section, American Society for Quality Control. Los Angeles: Urgo & Associates.

Index

READER FEEDBACK
Fax to ASQ Quality Press Acquisitions: 414-272-1734

Comments and Areas for Improvement:
Nimble Documentation®

Please give us your comments, feedback, and suggestions for making this book more useful. We believe in the importance of continuous improvement and in meeting your needs. Your comments will help determine what improvements can be made in all ASQ Quality Press books.

Please share your opinion by circling the number below:

Ratings of the book	Needs Work		Satisfactory		Excellent	Comments
Stucture, flow, and logic	1	2	3	4	5	
Content, ideas, and information	1	2	3	4	5	
Style, clarity, ease of reading	1	2	3	4	5	
Held my interest	1	2	3	4	5	
Met my overall expectations	1	2	3	4	5	

I read the book because:

The best part of the book was:

The least satisfactory part of the book was:

Other suggestions for improvement:

General comments:

Thank you for your feedback. If you do not have access to a fax machine, please mail this form to:
ASQ Quality Press, 611 East Wisconsin Avenue, P.O. Box 3005, Milwaukee, WI 53201-3005   Phone: 414-272-8575